29 and Counting

A Chick's Guide to Turning 30

JULIE TILSNER

CB

CONTEMPORARY BOOKS

Library of Congress Cataloging-in-Publication Data

Tilsner, Julie.
    29 and counting : a chick's guide to turning 30 / Julie Tilsner.
       p.   cm.
    Includes bibliographical references.
    ISBN 0-8092-2937-4
    1. Young women—Psychology.   2. Women—Psychology.   I. Title.
HQ1206.T48   1998
305.242—dc21   97-46613
                                            CIP

To Anna Florence

Cover illustration copyright © Margaret Spengler
Cover and interior design by Mary Lockwood

Published by Contemporary Books
A division of NTC/Contemporary Publishing Group, Inc.
4255 West Touhy Avenue, Lincolnwood (Chicago), Illinois 60646-1975 U.S.A.
Copyright © 1998 by Julie Tilsner
Printed in the United States of America
International Standard Book Number: 0-8092-2937-4
    9 0 DSH/DSH 0 1 0

CONTENTS

PREFACE

So, Like . . .

Let me look at you. You're looking pretty good for a chick of your age. I can see it in your clothes, your face, your attitude—you're in those prime and indeterminate years between your mid-20s and your early 30s. If it weren't for that slightly worried look in your eye and the way you're leaving thumb prints in this book, I might never guess that you're up for turning 30 fairly soon.

Sorry. I made you wince.

Turning 30 could be a very touchy subject with you. Or it could be merely a curious accident on the highway o' life that gives you the willies as you speed by. However you feel about it, chances are you're feeling something. Because, let's just face it, no chick—no matter how reasonable she is, no matter how above it all she fancies herself—ever expects the age of 30 to come for her.

Hey, it happens to the best of us. Even though back when you were 19 the idea of ever getting as old as 30 seemed as likely as you agreeing to wear platform shoes, somehow it's come to pass. And platform shoes are, I'm sure you've noticed, very in again.

Not too very long ago, you yourself held all the worst stereo-types about 30-year-olds. They were those who were to be pitied, the chicks in the sensible shoes, the ones with the resigned look in their eyes. Sure, you knew one or two chicks who'd turned 30 who were still reasonably hip, but they surely couldn't be the norm. You'd always just assumed that some chemical change took place in your late 20s that turned you from a vibrant youth into a plodding adult overnight. Such a fate would never befall you. You ranted at *thirtysomething* every week (though you watched it without fail) because it seemed to embody the worst of the age group. You swore at the top of your lungs that you would never be such swinish yuppae as that lot when you were in your 30s. But back then you were safely ensconced in your early or mid-20s, or younger. Perhaps you were still in high school. So you could swear these things in the absolute comfort of your own certainty that you yourself would never actually turn 30, God forbid.

But it's happening. You're going to be 30 and you wonder how you got yourself in this situation. What happened to your 20s? Didn't you just graduate from college a few years ago? Weren't you going to have accomplished a few things by now? Written that novel, maybe? Or started your own business? Of course you probably thought you'd be married by now, and you certainly figured you'd have the kid thing in order. But here you are nearing 30 and you haven't gotten around to any of those things yet. A lot of you don't even have a reliable date for Friday night.

What's really got you peeved is the fact that you care at all. You've always thought of yourself as a chick of substance. An independent thinker. You've never been one to give much thought to fashion or the Rachel cut. You've certainly steered clear of those silly women's magazine tests like "How to Keep your Man at 20, 30, and 40" (OK, so you took one recently while waiting for your annual pap smear). You'd like to think you know the difference between what's real and what's marketing. You know perfectly well that age is just a number, and that you're only as old as you feel, etc., etc., ad nauseam.

And yet this birthday is different. The idea of leaving your 20s and entering your 30s has you just . . . a little bit . . . out of sorts. In fact, you're really pretty alarmed at the whole idea. The dramatic among you might even admit to being a tad bipolar over it. Nothing like this has ever happened to you before, damn it. And you'd like an explanation.

Welcome to 30. Turning it knocks just about everyone off their dot. At least for a little while. Even the chicks you look askance at with envy, the ones with everything you want—the boffo jobs, the last good men, or the authentic Prada wedges— they're chewing their expensive French-tip nails in distress too. If there's any one basic truth to turning 30, it's that no matter where you're at by this point, it's not where you want to be.

I feel your pain.

Just three short years ago, I was in your clogs, turning 30 before I was ready and completely messed up about it. I'm much better now, thank you, but when you read about the mental cartwheels I did between 29 and 31, you'll regard me with a strange blend of awe and pity. But truly I say unto you, now that I'm officially in my mid-30s, I'm a noted authority on turning 30 and surviving.

I can confirm that things aren't as bleak as they seem when you're 29-and-counting. I can talk at length about various forms of denial and their relative effectiveness. I can tell you that contrary to what you thought when you were 23, just about everything gets a hell of a lot better for a girl after 30. In fact, I can tell you a lot of things about turning 30 that you might be in the mood to hear right about now.

Hence the first ever *Chick's Guide to Turning 30*.

ACKNOWLEDGMENTS

A good girlfriend of mine once pulled out a bestselling book that she could have written but did not and asked me to read the acknowledgments page.

It said, "My undying thanks to Binky."

My friend looked grim. "I could die a fulfilled life," said she, "if I ever got to give my undying thanks to Binky in a book acknowledgment."

Binky, for those of you fortunate enough to dwell far from New York publishing circles, is the superagent Amanda "Binky" Urban.

I've never met Binky, and I'm reasonably sure I never will. But I must extend my undying thanks to her anyway because it was she who inspired an article in the *New York Observer*, titled "Baby Binkys," about hot, up-and-coming literary agents in New York under the age of 35. That article of course included Elizabeth Ziemska, my agent and uber-chick, who immediately saw that the world needed a *Chick's Guide to Turning 30*, and fast. Aw, shucks, I guess this is my roundabout way of saying, "Thanks, Liz!"

Thanks as well to all the women who let me invade their personal space and interview them. Special thanks to all the chicks at *Business Week* who cornered me that summer near my 30th birthday and set me straight: Linda Himelstein, Joni Warner, Pam Black, Kathleen "Mad Dog" Madigan, Joni Danaher, Cathy Arnst, Amy Dunkin, Lauren Stockbower, Dede Depke, Anne Murray, Ronnie Weil, Francesca Messina, and Claire Worley. You were right. You told me so.

More recently, Katharine Mieszkowski and Diane Sussman have both been promised my firstborn son for their vast amounts of encouragement, creativity, and liquid refreshment. If I ever have one, they will just have to share.

Thanks to Matthew Carnicelli who laughed at my proposal, my manuscript, and my jokes on the phone, and who manhandled me with the perfect blend of coddling and severity. Also to his assistant, Jenna DiGregorio, who identified with the whole book even though she's an entire decade younger than I am.

A very low bow to Mom and Dad, of course, who with patient good humor continue to help me pay the rent occasionally. A salacious wink to Luke, who has kept me happy and well-fed for several years now, and a big sloppy wet one to Annie, who decided to coincide with this whole thing.

INTRODUCTION

30 Happens

I am no social scientist. But I have enough girlfriends (and enough journalistic training) to dig a pattern when I see one. Everything I've heard, listening to girlfriend after girlfriend moaning over the phone about how she's sure to die childless now that she's almost 30 and has not had a decent date in two years, leads me to conclude that there is a distinct pattern to getting over turning 30. These are five stages that can happen in no particular order, but to keep the chaos of the universe at bay, I am listing them here as Fear, Denial, Bargaining (The Lists), The Countdown, and The Great Beyond.

Let's pretend this is a magazine or a website and synopsize, synopsize, synopsize. It would read something like this:

The Five Stages of Turning 30

Fear

It dawns on you that, wait a minute, Time did not grant you a divine Exemption. You too will age, and yes, you too will one day be 30. Fear hits different women at different times—

sometimes as early as 22, sometimes as late as 31, but most often on or after the 25th birthday. And there are lots of things to be afraid of, right? Well, yeah, of course. We list 'em here.

Denial

Just don't think about it and it will go away, right? Wrong! Has that strategy ever worked? And in this case, if you ignore it for too long you'll just wake up in the final throes of 29, and where will that leave you? The denial stage is when a lot of women start lying about their age, something they swore in their 20s they'd never do. Denial is also the reason so many chicks I know in their mid-20s decide to rush off and get something pierced. . . .

In any case, the denial stage doesn't last for long, because the laws of biology dictate that you will turn 30 no matter what you do, and so barring an act of God, you'll either have to get used to the idea and use it to your best advantage or pull a Kurt Cobain, which is a little melodramatic for your age (although look what it did for Courtney Love's career). Besides, do you really want to miss your sexual peak? I didn't think so.

Bargaining (The Lists)

Big lists, small lists, lists scribbled in your secret journal or lists written up at work to be printed out as a pie chart on the color laser printer. They are lists of accomplishments, material possessions, dreams, or goals. The only qualifier is that you've told yourself you have to have them by 30. Everybody does them. Twenty-something magazine *Swing* recently published a list of its own called "100 Things You Must Do Before You're 30" (including instructions to dance on a bar and get insurance). Tragically, though, most of what's on *your* list are big-ticket items (like husbands, kids, or bestselling novels . . . although health insurance ain't a bad idea, either). Not the sort of thing you can run down and splurge on (at least you hope not). Brooding over lists like this, then, tends to lead to the realization that attaching such accomplishments to an arbitrary age is a waste of time. But it does get your darkest wants and needs out into the light of day, which also might motivate you to take one or two items from your list and run with them.

The Countdown

This officially starts the eve of your 29th birthday. No matter what kind of celebration you have (and there are so many kinds to choose from), your internal odometer will have clicked over. It can not be helped. No matter how well adjusted you think you're being about this whole thing, rest assured that for the entire year, an irritating little whine of a voice will be there to remind you, "Five months and counting before you're 30." We look at all the "firsts" you can expect to notice now, as well as all the biggies you were supposed to have accomplished well before this year. Then we explain why you can forgo them for a few more years.

The Great Beyond

The day of your 30th birthday you're going to wake up so relieved you'll think you've just won the lottery. Now you can get on with the next 50 or 60 years of your life and never worry about turning 30 again. The best part is: you're going to see how much better life is now that you're old enough to know better but still young enough to do it anyway. We take a long look at the new realities of your career, your confidence, dating and the 30-something chick, and your new sexual peak.

Pretty tidy, huh? Didn't think you could break down such a milestone into five easy-to-remember compartments, did you? Well, it can be done because the world loves tidy little lists (that's why chicks who are approaching 30 make so many of them). And it can be done because it's that *fin de siecle* time again and any one of us can proclaim herself a prophet if she wants to. Besides, nobody else has written anything on this topic that doesn't involve skin cream. So it's all up for wild, personal interpretation as far as I'm concerned. (But I do mention skin cream. It's in the section about wrinkles.)

I'll tell you something else. Just so you don't have to read the last page of this book to see what the main point is: once you turn 30, they couldn't pay you to be 22 again. Women are pretty much unanimous on that one. Even the ones whose livelihoods depend on them being pretty young thangs. (Remember, there's absolutely nothing wrong with looking like a 22-year-old, if that's what makes you happy or pays the rent. And I'd like to personally thank every grocery store clerk who's demanded to see my ID recently when I'm buying wine for dinner. God bless you all, from the bottom of my 33-year-old heart.)

Don't Just Stand There Browsing, Buy the Damn Book

Why do you need this book? Because it's the only book with the audacity to guide you through the biggest birthday of your life thus far. Inasmuch as anyone can offer a guide on how to age, I purport to do so for you, through a lot of personal anecdotes, interviews with other chicks (some just like you, others way more gorgeous or successful), and a smattering of actual experts on topics such as marriage and physical health. A veritable cornucopia of yuks and empathetic nods await you. The book is arranged rather along the lines of your own pre-30 panic. I weave my own story throughout, largely in an attempt to make you feel at ease—because it's a rare bird who would approach 30 with as much trepidation as I did. Then I tell you what exactly you're afraid of (and there's lots of stuff here, so you may want to break out your St.-John's-wort tea). From there I examine denial, bargaining, and creation of the infamous lists, the countdown of your 29th year, followed by the grand denouement of the big day itself, which is usually sickeningly anticlimactic. But you have to read that far, first. Finally, I let you in on the good news: all the stuff you can expect to get better in your 30s—stuff like your career, your dating skills, your sexual prowess, and your overall confidence.

In short, you who are about to turn 30 are very lucky girls.

A Note on Language

Please note, girls, that I used the term *chick* in the best colloquial sense. Ditto the terms *girls*, *ladies*, *girlfriends*, etc. To paraphrase the great goddess Cynthia Heimel, author of *Sex Tips for Girls*: we can call each other chicks, dames, skirts, whatever, but God help any man who does.

Need more mood setting? OK. Pretend you're sitting with me in a cafe somewhere on a Sunday afternoon. There are caffeinated beverages on order and we've got a bet on whether our Greek god of a waiter is gay or straight and every one of us has some scandalous dish to impart. This is serious chick talk.

Top 10 Myths About Turning 30

1. The night of your 30th birthday, your old, carefree youthful self will suddenly and without explanation evaporate into the void.

2. If you wake up at all, you will feel old.

3. If you don't feel old, you will certainly look old.

4. You should have married that last guy.

5. You're probably infertile now anyway.

6. Your career has stalled forever.

7. You will never start your own company.

8. You will never write that novel/screenplay/sitcom treatment.

9. Nobody will ever use the term *wunderkind* and your name in the same sentence.

10. You will have to start acting like a grown-up now.

So if you're not in the mood or you're feeling a mite more serious than the rest of us, kindly put this book down and proceed back to the women's studies section. OK? I mean it.

Who am I to speak of such things? Girlfriend, nobody freaked out over turning 30 more than I did. In a nutshell, I worked, connived, schemed, did whatever I had to do my entire 20s to get to where I was at 30. And when I finally got there I looked around, pronounced myself a miserable, wretched failure, and proceeded to dismantle the whole mess. And of course I went through the five stages of turning 30, but I did it more like Fear, The Countdown, Bargaining (The Lists), and then when I was already 30, Denial and The Great Beyond. But you probably want the whole juicy dish, don't you? Well then. One more reason to read this book. What were you doing this Saturday night anyway?

My point exactly.

1 FEAR

What Do You Mean I'm Not 24 Anymore?

Thirty looks great when you're 50.
But it's scary as hell when you're 29.

Darian O'Toole, former KBIG show
DJ philosophizing on her 30th
birthday morning show

What, Me Worry?

I've always been a worrier. Ask my mom. When it was time for my first day at kindergarten, I woke up before daylight, got myself dressed, and then tried to rouse Mom to take me so I wouldn't be late. She assured me that it was far too early to be getting ready to go to school. Since I couldn't tell time yet, I had no choice but to rely on her and she couldn't be trusted to take my first day of school as seriously as I took it. So I had to wake her every half-hour just to be sure. I remember well the feeling of panic boiling up in me as I padded back to my room to wait another few minutes.

I was certain that things were going to go monumentally wrong and that my future was slipping away before it had even begun. This kind of fretting of mine has hung on to this very day.

At 22 I had my first inkling that time was moving on. I wasn't quite out of college, but when I compared myself to girl-friends who hadn't gone, I felt as if I'd been wasting time. They seemed as if they were accomplishing actual things. They were getting promoted. Some were having families. One in particu-lar had started doing commercials while in high school and had now progressed to small parts in feature films. I, meanwhile, had been sitting in Microeconomics 101 and Poli Sci 6 for the last four years. "What have I done with my life so far?" I brooded, head in hands. I couldn't point to any one thing I had accomplished in my life. Of course I was 22 years old. Somebody should have slapped me at the time.

At 25 my friends and coworkers at the small weekly paper I worked for gave me no less than three chocolate cakes, a clock that operated on potato-power, and dozens of cards, many of which helpfully pointed out the obvious: "Five More Years to 30!" Again I wandered around in a daze. "I'm a quarter of a century old!" How, I fretted, had I come from 18 to this so quickly? I was worried but not too much. There seemed to be time. I was just on the verge of doing something with my life; I could feel it. Thirty still seemed far enough away not to pose a real threat to my well-being.

The next five years went by in a blur eaten up by work, grad-uate school, the search for work, and more work. Trying to build a career is a very effective way of passing time, almost as good as doing nothing. By the time I looked up and took stock of my surroundings, I was right where I had never expected to be: 29 years old and counting.

Nope. Nothing was as I'd planned as my 30th year edged up on me. To my mind, 30-year-olds were grown-ups. They owned things like houses or late-model cars or mutual funds. They were married, and some of them even had (gasp!) children. This proved that they had gotten their lives, jobs, and priorities straight.

Good thing nobody in whose circles I lurked fell into this category, because I certainly didn't. In fact, despite all my efforts to the contrary, life around my 30th birthday sucked. On paper it looked OK, even kind of glamorous. I'd accomplished, in a sort of a technical way, the dreams I'd set for myself in college. I was living in New York City. I worked as an editor at a major magazine. I had lots of friends and never ever went for more than four weeks between dates. So what was the problem?

I hadn't written my novel yet, damn it. That's what the problem was. Nor had I gotten a short story published in *The New Yorker*, as I'd planned to by now back when I started writing them at 17. I hadn't met Mr. Right yet either. (I'd left Mr. Right in California when I'd moved to New York.) I certainly didn't have a baby yet and, gauging the stunning array of assholes I now tended to date, wouldn't be having one anytime soon. Although I worked more than full-time, I never had enough to even dent my Visa bill, much less the $15,000 in student loans I enjoyed thanks to my one year of graduate school. I slept on a futon in one room of a two-room apartment I rented with another chick in similar circumstances. I had an astounding $200 in savings (and I was proud to have saved that much). I routinely called home for small cash infusions to pay a dental bill here, a gap in the rent there. As 30 loomed, I was a debt-ridden wretch who hated my job *and* my apartment and was in no way fit to join the ranks of adults. I grew increasingly morose wondering what had happened to those eight years between college and now, and how it was I still lived like a 19-year-old. More terrifying: Would I be able to remedy any of this before I woke up with 30 on the other side of me? No way.

My worrying had oozed over the perception wall to become something more desperate, more full-bodied. My worrying had metamorphosed into fear.

Am I alone in this? Somehow I think not. There are too many "Now You're 30" gag cards on the shelves of Hallmark stores across America. There are too many "100 Things You *Must* Do Before You're 30" lists being published by snide, glossy 20-something magazines. I know way too many chicks approaching 30—sensible girls all—who are boiling in this very soup of terror to know that I was not some singular oddball in need of therapy.

So if there has to be a first stage of turning 30, it's this: fear. If you doubt this for even a moment, ask yourself whether you felt like this back when you were turning 20. Didn't think so.

Lots of Fear

It's true that there's a lot to be afraid of in today's world. Downsizing, globalization, road rage. There's so much sturm und drang on those 500 channels (not including the Internet) that it's not surprising everything makes you jump. But this fear of turning 30 is a real pip. It's been growing since your 27th birthday or so. It seems to have a heft that, say, the fear of getting brain cancer from your cellular phone does not. It has real implications for your life, your future. This fear is personal.

Everyone has heard a turning-30 nightmare. They're like urban myths. Some, like the story about the guy who got early-onset Alzheimer's at 31, we prefer to discount out of hand along with rumors of giant mutant alligators in the sewer system. Others, however, are verifiable. And no less terrifying.

Darian O'Toole was horrified at the thought of turning 30 for some of these very same reasons. But at 29 she was a successful disc jockey with her own morning show in San Francisco, an agent, legions of adoring fans, and the really big bucks. Pictures of her, looking very young and hip with her long red hair and shit-eating grin, plastered the backs of buses all over town. When she decided to turn 30 on her show, it was declared a brilliant piece of radio production. Dozens of people, women and men, called in to calm her while she went through the five stages of turning 30 over the airwaves. It was great radio, I thought. (And what a great gal to profile for my book!) I called her producer and got a message through to Darian, who called me enthusiastically the next week. "I'd totally love to talk to you about turning 30," she said. "I'm still freaking out."

Two weeks later I went to call her and pin down the interview date. But of course, being me, I'd hopelessly lost the envelope I'd written her home phone number on. No matter, I thought, I'd just call the radio station. But when I called, the receptionist's voice turned cold. "She's no longer affiliated with the station," she said. Since last Wednesday.

Apparently (while I had been on Pluto, or some other dimension where there are no newspapers) another company had bought the station and executed a swift, brutal format change. Not a shaggy head from the former classic rock station survived the sweep, from the star morning-show host to the most humble of assistant producers. I was stricken.

I used every reporter tactic I could think of to find Darian O'Toole. I searched my pile of notes again and rummaged in the debris surrounding my computer. I checked information and scoured the phone book. I did Internet searches. I called other radio stations. Nothing. There was no sign of Darian O'Toole. She had turned 30. She'd gotten the boot from her job. And she had disappeared.

I'm sure she landed on her feet (after all, that's what agents are for). And flash-format changes are fairly routine in the radio biz. But I still get this crazy chill down my back whenever I think of her: mug on the back of a muni one day, vanished the next.

So yes, Virginia, there is reason to fear turning 30. While many would argue that it is irrational to be so afraid of just another birthday, many would also say that it can not be helped. So I say unto you: give in to the fear. You're powerless against it, so you may as well wallow deeply. Go on. Get in there and cover yourself with it. It'll make it much easier to progress through the next four stages of turning 30, and it will make fabulous dinner conversation when you're safe again in your early 30s and wondering what all the fuss was about.

On fear, Franklin D. Roosevelt said it best: "We have nothing to fear but fear itself," which was a great pep talk through real problems like the Depression but of little succor to American chicks who have nothing, really, to fear, except growing up, perhaps, and then after that, growing old.

A Caveat

Here's where I duck and cover myself against the onslaught of every single person over 30 who just read that last passage. Let me say for the record: *I know 30 does not constitute old age in any way.* And I know I will suffer derision from all the aging experts out there who are going to think I'm saying that 30 years old means over the hill when all I'm trying to say is that it means the hill is now in sight.

I know 30 isn't old because women of our mother's generation were all too busy chasing their 10-year-olds to worry about turning 30. I know this because 70-year-olds still chuck us on the chin and call us sweetie. I know that most 40-year-olds don't even get the point of this book.

But I also know that every chick under the age of 30 *does not* know this. And this is why you're reading this book. You need to be reassured that your fear of turning 30 is absolutely normal. So normal, in fact, that it can be broken down and examined like a seventh grade biology project. So normal that not one of us is going to snicker at you for any of this. Your fears about turning 30 do not make you a bimbo. I promise.

Fear of a New Demographic

Nope. Thirty is not old. What it is, however, is the first whiff of old. It's the very first signpost in our own aging. (When I start sounding too New Agey, feel free to slap me.) In the lexicon of aging, there are several stages of "old." There is the young old, and there is the old old. What 30 is, seems to me, is the very first inkling of old. Even though you may still be into raving all night and you may dye your hair unnatural shades of red, even if you're taking great pains to maintain your slacker status and wearing your grunge on your sleeve, when your 30th birthday comes a-callin', suddenly you feel like a fraud. Bad enough society expects all 30-year-olds to start acting like grown-ups. But you tend to agree with them.

"It's not that I feel so old," says Trisha Szajak, 31, who not so long ago was singing in a thrash metal band and showing the men how to drink like men. "It's just that I'm probably a little too old for *that*."

When did you first realize that you weren't officially the youth of America anymore? Was it the first time you tuned into the college station and had no idea what the hell kinda crap they were playing? Was it the time you passed your old high school and the kids all looked . . . like children? (They probably threw things at you too, the little punks.) Or was it more recently, when your younger brother invited you to his dorm party but the idea of passing the beer bong with a bunch of 21-year-olds made you glaze over. Maybe it was as simple as having to check the 30–45 age box on the warranty for your new Cuisinart because it was the first box listed. Nobody under 30 would ever buy a Cuisinart.

However it happens, the epiphany that you're not part of the younger generation comes as a shock. After all, we've been the mass media's target for, oh, nearly 30 years now, or exactly as long as TV has been craftily targeting young people. When *Sesame Street* aired its first broadcast in 1969, we were there, the three-to-six-year-olds crying because it wasn't all in cartoons. We had Big Wheels. We watched every new season of *The Brady Bunch* and *Happy Days* and *The Six Million Dollar Man* sprawled in our avocado-colored bean bag chairs along with all our friends in our parents' sunken, teak-lined dens. When cable TV was in its primitive stages, Pete Townshend urgently told us, "I want my MTV," and we, being impressionable teenagers, immediately agreed, and turned to the new music video channel in droves. Remember that song by Kim Wilde, "Kids in America"? (Wu-OH!) That was us, too. How could we think of ourselves as anything else but perpetually young?

But then the day comes when the first high school kid refers to us as "ma'am." We start realizing that we saw *Star Wars* when it came out the first time . . . 20 years ago . . . and we were sentient, babysitting, teenagers! For most of your life only adults used phrases like "I remember when" and "Fifteen years ago. . . ." But now you too can pull an old, warped copy of Pink Floyd's *The Wall* from a box in your parents' garage and reminisce: "I remember when this came out . . . 17 years ago." (I want to cry even now.)

More clues you're in a new demographic: Define "ambient" music. Can't do it, can you? Probably can't dance to it, either. And do you know the reason every single kid over the age of 10 wears a beeper clipped to his or her pants these days? Me neither.

Ladies, we're not the youth they're talking to anymore.

I'm OK about this now, understand. But when I was in the very dying embers of my 20s, this realization was kind of hard to take.

Fear of Growing Up

But let's cut to the chase here. Turning 30 means a lot of different things to different people, but the bottom line is this: we are terrified of aging. Lurking in the heart of every 29-year-old chick is the fear, however distant, of one day growing old. But more imminent is perhaps a worse fear, that of growing up. Growing old and growing up. To do the former, one must first accomplish the latter. And as everyone knows, nothing about aging, in any form, is thought of as any fun. At least not in this country.

Even though our generation didn't coin the phrase "Never trust anyone over 30," the idea behind it has been floating around in this boomer-designed culture for so long that it's almost an inborn notion. *They* are over 30. You know: the grown-ups. The establishment. Not us.

Until now, poor dears.

Let's be clear about this. Thirty is absolutely not "just another birthday." The cold hard fact remains that the day we turn 30 is the day we're dragged kicking and screaming into adulthood. Ready or not.

Nobody wants to grow up. Even the chick who possesses certain accoutrements of adulthood—say she's married, or owns a late-model car, or maybe she actually has savings in a 401K plan (and can define what that is). She isn't too keen on the idea of having to grow up either. That's for other people. Your Aunt Hildy. Your dentist.

"But I don't wanna be a grown-up" goes the whine. And indeed, why would we want to? Grown-ups are roundly mocked by everyone in our culture, even other grown-ups. David Letterman, for example, has made quite a tidy living mocking grown-ups, all the while refusing to grow up himself. And his 30th birthday is ancient history.

Besides, the stuff usually associated with grown-updom is mundane and bourgeois, so of course we want it desperately.

Grown-Up Checklist

Take a minute right now to itemize your grown-up checklist. Does any of it sound like any fun? No, it does not. Especially not for chicks of our generation, in this particular country, at this point in time.

✦ A mortgage. Hmm. Never seemed to make Mom or Dad deliriously happy to be alive.

✦ Kids. Your parents had them (duh). You don't. Nobody you know does either. Kids generally require a life and/or stability and/or a husband or other mate, which, taken together, is just asking too much.

✦ Savings/investments. Please God, let the market crash already so I can go bottom sucking.

✦ Health insurance. Once again, a nice, old-fashioned foil of adulthood taken for granted by our parents and grandparents. Also, thank you, by our temp agencies.

✦ A station wagon. In today's parlance, these are now called Land Rovers, and they cost just about what your parents paid for their first house.

✦ Lawn furniture. Doesn't look good on a fire escape.

And yet, most of us can not afford these things. So we continue to malign them whenever we can.

See? Apart from being silly, it's also futile. What would growing up mean in real terms? It would mean we'd have to stop moving every year. It would mean having to buy a real bed and putting the old futon out of its misery. It would mean having to intentionally purchase a new couch instead of using the one you found on the corner. With requirements like these, is it any wonder the 30-something writer Sandra Tsing Loh refers to us as the Ikea generation?

Here's a better example. *When Harry Met Sally* is my all-time favorite film, required viewing within the first month of any new relationship. So I feel I can quote from it to make a point.

Sally calls Harry up one night in tears. Alarmed, he shows up at her apartment to find her sobbing. The man she'd broken up with some time ago to little effect has just informed her that he's engaged to be married. Suddenly, she falls completely apart. Her worst fears have forced their way out of her dark, cozy subconscious and into full light of day. "I'm gonna be 40!" she shrieks to Harry, who points out that she won't be 40 for another eight years. "Yeah, but it's there," she cries. "It's just sitting out there like some big dead end."

Who among us doesn't see this scene and shiver? Who the hell wants to be 40?

Fear of Becoming Them

But tragically, we all gotta go sometime, and regardless of how we feel about growing up at the moment, it's probably going to happen anyway. It's happening right now, in a million subtle ways. Nature in her wisdom has provided many crafty hormonal changes to temper our spastic, radical selves into more reasoned versions. And it never happens in one big mind-changing spurt so that you could actually do some quick before-

and-after comparison studies and launch a counterattack. No. It creeps up on you until it has you in its death grip, and by then you've developed a taste for John Tesh recordings. At least this tends to happen in flocks, so you're never without understanding company (assuming you hang out with people your own age or older).

Watch any group of friends for the inevitable trickle before the landslide and you'll see what happens for yourself. One girlfriend up and marries. Then another one does. Then the first one has a baby. Then a third girlfriend ties the knot, and before you know it, the whole lot of you are having dinner parties and getting to bed by a sensible hour. Suddenly, the idea of going to a club until the wee hours is about as appealing as cold tuna on toast. You would much rather stay home with your sig oth and watch *Toy Story* for the third time rather than venture out to a flick (where you'd have to pay $8.50 *and* look for parking). New Year's Eve parties start to resemble the most civilized of salons, with every lampshade unmolested. I've seen this happen. I've experienced it myself. It's really not so bad. But then, I'm almost 34. It's much too late for me.

This isn't to say that the inevitable downward spiral into adulthood means next year we'll be signing up for PTA bake sale monitor when we'd rather be out at a perpetual cocktail hour with our *beaux du jour*. Reaching the full flower of adulthood can take years. Some chicks manage to forestall it well into their 40s. Nor am I necessarily saying that becoming a grown-up is all that bad. (You start to save on car insurance, for example, after 35). But a gal shouldn't be in a hurry. We all know, after all, that 30 is the official dividing line between youth and adulthood. Between us and *them*.

If perpetual youth is paramount to your continued happy

existence on this earth, then by all means feel free to hide the truth from your younger peers. But be forewarned: thirty is a self-policing age. Consider the kids playing hippie panhandler on Haight Street in San Francisco. Even they know the difference between a 20-year-old playing counterculture hipster and a 30-year-old doing the same thing. Everyone knows there's something wrong with you when you haven't gotten your act together by 30. (Those 10 years turn you from a wild and carefree youth into a vagrant.) "You can still live at home and be full of angst if you're 22," says one chick I know. "But once you're 30, you're just a loser."

It's no easier for chicks who've gotten a little further down on their To Do in Life list. Take Nicole Gorham, 29, a high school basketball coach. She's married to a nice guy. They have a nice house (OK, so she hates the neighborhood, this ain't a fairy tale here) and they have a very cute toddler named Will. How does she feel about turning 30? "I don't wanna get old!" she howls whenever the topic is brought up. I've reminded her gently that 30, put in perspective, isn't really old. "It is when you teach high school girls," she growls. "They listen to music I've never heard before and use words I don't understand. And whenever I hear a song I like on the radio and start rocking out, they laugh at me."

Fear of the Music Gap

Music is the great dividing line between us and them. Always has been. Always will be. Just as Grampa was galled by rock and roll and Mom was galled by grunge, so too are we scratching our heads at whatever it is the college kids are listening to these days.

I hate to point this out, but unless you work as a nightclub DJ, the kind of music most of us listened to in our heyday is now fodder for classic rock stations across America. Can any of you tell me, for example, just what the hell Jungle is? I kind of know what trip hop sounds like (as distinct from hip hop), but the only reason I can define old school is because I recognize a few of the songs from my childhood AM radio listening days. The artists' names on the Top 10 pop chart these days might as well be Sanskrit.

Maybe this realization hadn't hit until someone invited you to one of those silly 80s parties. You know the kind—wear a skinny tie or a muscle-T or anything with pink-and-grey checks on it. You were just scrounging around for any old remaining Go-Gos or Adam Ant CDs when somebody tells you that you can get all that stuff on a "New Wave 80s" compilation CD from K-Tel for only $9.99. That's $9.99. Operators are standing by. Gulp. Your youth has become bad daytime television commercials.

Or worse, perhaps a younger coworker will remind you of the growing schism between what you listened to and what she listens to. Like when I went to the 24th birthday picnic of a coworker recently. She pulled out the soundtrack to a recent movie about the 10-year high school reunion of two chicks. It featured songs I hadn't heard in years, ones that brought on alarming flashbacks. But that wasn't the bad part. That came when my friend began to bounce up and down to The Knack's "My Sharona," a song very popular when I was 15 or 16, then featured on another movie soundtrack. "God," she reminisced, "I used to love this song when I was in grade school!"

Nothing ruins my day like being reminded that today's high school freshmen weren't even born when I graduated.

But I never thought I'd get old enough to be left perplexed by somebody else's music. Even when I was 16 and my tastes ran mostly to Journey and Police records, I was willing to admit that some of that Big Band music I'd heard on a movie sound-track was kind of fun, and one or two of my Mom's classical tapes had some merit. Even late into my 20s, I'd marvel at adults who didn't see Kurt Cobain's genius. But, like so many other epiphanies I had while traveling during my 30th year, I was to experience for myself the widening musical gap between me and them.

I was on Cyprus, hanging out with a bunch of English scuba divers I'd met on a ferry to Greece (a story for another time, ladies). They spent their days working and their nights party-ing in a manner I found alarming in its extremes. This I chalked up to the fact that they were (a) English, and so by genetic constitution able to consume far more alcohol than I could ever hope or want to, and (b) on average more than 10 years my junior.

Every evening they'd converge in someone's rented living room, break out several liters of some deadly proof spirit, pop a homemade cassette into the boom box, and begin gyrating wildly to the most obnoxious, melody-free white noise I'd ever heard in my life. It was known as techno.

BAM BAM BAM BAM BAM BAM BAM BAM BAM BAM BAM duh BAM! It went on and on all night long, and the divers and their ilk were transfixed. They'd swing their hair and throw their hands into the air and undulate and shake their arses for what seemed like epochs. I sat in the corner, nursing my first (and only) glass of hard liquor and tried to feel what, besides the driving beat, they were dancing to. I've been known to keep a beat, but the same one for two hours? Then

I learned that half the appeal was a drug, Ecstasy, which had to be ingested to appreciate the full glorious effect of techno. I'd heard of the drug years ago, right about the time I was phasing out of my recreational drug use. At that point, Ecstasy was en vogue among ultrahip gay circles in San Francisco and considered very hard to procure if you didn't have the right connections. Needless to say, I didn't have the right connections, and so never had the pleasure of sampling the drug.

But "E" was all the rage in England, and so, it turns out, was raving—a sort of huge, roving dance fest where E-soaked kids danced rapturously to this background din all weekend long and returned home remembering nothing. Raving was the defining moment for British youth, they told me. "It's like you're having a conversation with the music," said one. "Like you're interacting with it, like you're part of it."

Oh.

I tried to tell myself that it was a cultural difference. But it wasn't that at all. It was an age difference. I didn't get it. I didn't like the music. I didn't have any interest in losing a weekend, and let's just face it, I was a good 10 years older than anyone there and I couldn't seem to drink more than one glass of their fine rum before falling out of my chair. I was a strange old bird. And who'd invited me, anyway?

Fear and Loathing and the Cult of Youth

Where did this fear and loathing of adulthood come from? After all, with college and graduate school and travel and years of singlehood, chicks in America get to enjoy an extended adolescence far longer than chicks in most countries. When the time comes for us to join those ranks, why is the dirge music playing in the background? Why do we rend our clothing and gnash our teeth? Let me be so bold as to posit that these sentiments came from the boomers themselves, they who would not grow up.

In case you hadn't noticed, America is the land of the free and the home of the youth cult. It's a sick culture when we attach the greatest value to money and youth, even though the natural order of things seems to dictate that when you have a lot of one you have not much of the other. But there it is, on every billboard and in every magazine: beautiful young people living the good life with other beautiful young people, the emphasis always on the young. Even the models for denture ads or retirement homes look about 40. The message we get from the day we are born is clear: youth, beauty, and money rank above all else in our culture, far above wisdom, modesty, or, say, temperance. Why would any kid want to be president one day when she can aspire to be a supermodel instead and make so much more money? We never have to worry about the youth thing for about 30 years, then whammo! We can't even be surly youths anymore about society's obsession with youth, beauty, and money.

But what do we expect from a nation of immigrants? Young, hardy, adventurous souls always pushing toward the new and the untested. In a society like this, the old represented all that's worth running away from. The traditions from the old country weren't worth keeping. From the earliest days of this country, the mind-set was away from the past, away from those who had lived through it, and toward the new and exciting.

After World War II, with the popularization of new gizmos (like the TV) that could propel ideas and social norms to larger and larger audiences, the idea of old continued its downward slide. Anything old-fashioned—including people—just wasn't fashionable. It was onward and upward, toward the American Dream! New tract homes! New cars! New science! Tupperware! Who wanted to listen to all those depressive Depression-era folks, anyway? It was all going along so innocently. And then we came up against the boomers and their youth movement.

Ah yes, the boomers. Those millions born between the years of 1946 and 1964. It was their visions, their love affair with themselves, that soon infiltrated the porous popular culture. (Let me just add here, for the record, that while I, born in 1964, am technically a boomer, I disavow any and all association with them, their tastes, mores, paychecks, and proclivity to Land Rovers. I expect to starve along with you younger chicks when they actually succeed in cutting Social Security.) Anyway, when the boomers hit their 20s, "Never trust anyone over 30" practically became a national mantra. It was the full flower of the youth movement, with all the attendant music, fashions, and political activism. Every one of them sure they were going to change the world, save it from the square old farts who'd been ruining it until then. As much as we're all sick and tired of hearing of it, the '60s and early '70s must have been pretty heady times. Oh, to be young and beautiful and full of idealism for a brave new world. I wouldn't know much about it myself, being all of three years old during the Summer of Love. But I do know this: the boomers have been notoriously loath to let go of this golden youth of theirs. And this has helped create a society that is not only afraid of aging, but will take extreme measures to avoid it if at all possible.

Witness the many new and exciting ways to stay young, assuming you can pay for the privilege. Middle-aged men invented the trophy wife, and middle-aged women retaliated by "inventing" the face-lift, boob job, tummy tuck, and lipo-suction. There's been the nationwide health kick. There are exotic, invigorating teas. There is Deepak Chopra.

Staying young, in fact, has become a raging beast of an industry. In the last 15 years, plastic surgery has become the fastest-growing segment of the medical profession, and among the most lucrative (although I found it telling when a girlfriend of mine at Yale Medical School said that to preserve their respect amongst peers, nobody would ever admit to specializing in cosmetic surgery until they had to). The media is always telling us how these makers of sunblock, denture creams, and new butts are salivating as the first of the boomers start to *really* age; and books on how to feel young, look young, or hell, how to live forever and ever and become the undead hit the best-seller lists routinely.

In light of these amusing cultural realities, you who are about to turn 30 can expect no sympathy from the masses. Seek succor from the usual aging wonks and you'll be reminded that 30 is not old, thank you very much, so stop being silly and vain and get your act together right this instant. This senti-ment is born out by the dearth of anything substantial written about the topic. On the trauma of turning 30, the boomer-heavy mass media is strangely silent. Lots of books written about turning 40. And you can't swing a pair of bifocals with-out hitting a book or article about boomers turning 50. How to keep young is the question of the '90s, it seems, so who are we to dither?

Previous generations didn't have this problem. For a variety of reasons, including economic ones, folks two or more gener-ations back sidled into adulthood as soon as they could and didn't seem to complain much about it. Yes, wars tend to make men out of boys. So do major economic depressions. But until the '60s, most people accepted certain rites and rituals of adulthood and entered into them with a minimum of whining. People got married, had children, and bought homes because, well, because that's what was done. The men got jobs and the women had babies and everyone sort of muddled through as best they could.

Fear of Making a Choice ... Any Choice

Obviously, a hefty reason chicks of yore were lockstepped into motherhood, teaching, or nursing was because those were the three career choices in their entire bag of options. And even the teachers and nurses were expected to quit once they got married and had that first bambino.

And just as obviously, this ain't the case today. We've got choices, baby. We've got so many choices, not only about what we want to do careerwise, but also about how we want to live, who we want to live with, where we want to live, and what we want to wear while living there. It's why so many of us choose procrastination, or, in lieu of that, paralysis.

Our generation is particularly smothered by this. It's easy to spend the 10 years between college and your early 30s just tasting the diverse lifestyles available on this week's menu, and getting fired from an array of interesting, go-nowhere jobs. We, after all, were told that we could do anything we wanted, and indeed should follow our bliss wherever it led. (Allegedly, the money would follow.)

This wasn't always the case. In fact, for chicks, it absolutely was not the case until about a generation ago. To see how much things have changed in the last 20 years, read some of the popular literature on aging and social structures. Written in 1975, Gail Sheehy's ground-breaking bestseller *Passages* contains a section on entering the 30s that is almost incomprehensible to a 30-year-old chick today. The women Sheehy profiled were caught in a horrible double standard that was still in full effect despite the efforts of the fledgling women's movement. Their husbands, who were coming into their own in their careers, were starting to get bored with their housebound wives, wondering why they couldn't go out, get educated, maybe become a little more dynamic and exciting. But woe betide the women who tried to do just that, because their husbands also wanted them to remain devoted wives and mothers, and not dilute their primary function by trying to broaden their lives through education or work. I found that both parties realized the hypocrisy going on, but were clueless as to how to step beyond it. The women who were on their own, either through design or divorce, faced daunting institutional discrimination. Ask your moms if they could apply for their own credit card back in the '70s, when "head of household" always meant "male."

Thankfully, many of these women taught their daughters a different way. My mom got the first issue of *Ms.* magazine. (It had Wonder Woman on the front cover—and I, being seven years old, dutifully cut it all up for school projects.) I listened to Marlo Thomas's *Free to Be You and Me* and all that other stuff designed to make young girls aware that even though they were girls and all, they could be president of the United States one day if they really wanted to. (Well, OK, so even repressive Islamic states like Pakistan and conservative, heavily Catholic republics like Ireland have been a bit more progressive in that arena. But I still wear my "Hilary for President in 2000" pin.)

So when it came time for me to decide what I wanted to do when I grew up, I looked at the menu and was blinded by the sheer combinations of things I could opt for. I took the most obvious route: get a job, work my way up, see what happens. But a lot of chicks out there were not only blinded, they were paralyzed too.

"When I got out of college, I almost felt crushed by the expectation that I was supposed to *do* something great with myself," says Keri Burrett, 30. "But what? I could do anything, so consequently, I did none of it."

Actually, she did a lot: worked on a ranch in Colorado, taught English in Japan, traveled the country with her brother, and spent a few years as a flight attendant. Right now she's just begun work on her teaching credentials. "I'm starting all over again," she shrugs. "But I kind of like starting over all the time."

There are a lot of chicks out there who have come to the conclusion that too much choice isn't always a good thing. Not one of them, understand, wants to go back to the days of June Cleaver and Harriet Nelson. (Who could afford those pearls?) Nevertheless, a lot of us more indecisive souls have wondered what life would be like if we had five or six choices in life instead of five hundred. Or maybe we girls long for a clearer role to emerge in this era of third-wave feminism, although God knows what that would be. Lordy, I know this sounds like heresy, but these thoughts are out there. Please don't send Andrea Dworkin after me.

It's just that for all but the most myopic, focused chicks, the vast, uncharted freedom out there is terrifying. How does one choose between culinary school and the Peace Corps and a full-time, well-paying job? And if one does choose between them, how does one know she's chosen right? Especially when you're a foolish tyro of 22 or 23, wondering whether taking a year off to travel will ruin your job prospects or whether you should plunge right into law school like everybody else.

"It was much more mapped out for us in my generation," says Ann F. Caron, a psychologist and author of two books on youth and aging. "As a woman, you got married and had children. For us, 40 was the age we dreaded, because by then we'd already raised our children, and were wondering what we could do next."

We, on the other hand, are wondering what to do first.

The terror of making the wrong choice gave me the night sweats in the months leading up to my college graduation. The perfect job was out there for me—I could feel it!—the job that would catapult me into the stratosphere where I so desperately wanted to be. *But what if I didn't find out about it until it was too late?* What if there were two jobs offered, one at a small daily paper for slave wages and the other at a PR firm where I'd make enough to pay off my student loan? *What would I do?* Since my plan for world domination included a stint as a feature writer at some major metropolitan daily, I always opted for the slave-wage job, where I was supposed to go in order to work my way up. This was just another newspaper industry ruse designed to embitter young practitioners, and indeed, I never did get to write features for a major metro daily. So in retrospect, perhaps I should have paid off my student loans instead, because now I surely never will.

See how hard it is to make the right choice before you're 30? In general it's easier to ignore the whole choice conundrum for as long as possible.

But now it's last call. After college, when everyone last wanted to know what your plans were, any number of cute and/or impetuous answers, delivered with a shake of your curls, would do. Not so today. When you're 30 and people ask, "No, really, what do you do?" either have something legit to tell them or fend them off with a well-rehearsed and plausible lie. In the meantime, try to face the fact that it's time to make a choice. Any choice.

Les Choix

For some chicks, this pressure is actually something of a relief. Kelly Garton, 30, spent her 20s studying and traveling around the world teaching English as a second language. It was a handy postcollege plan, she recalls. "Whenever anyone asked me what I was going to do now that I'd graduated, I just told them, 'I'm traveling.' And that was that."

And that was that for a good long time too. She spent extended periods in Russia, Hungary, and Brazil. She'd return home to the States briefly for R & R, then fly off again. She came back for good in early 1995, when she was 27, and proceeded to pay her rent through a variety of odd jobs while trying to pinpoint just what it was exactly that she really wanted to do when she grew up.

"The 20s are a real dabbling time, for both genders," she says. "You just go along testing things out, seeing what there is, seeing what you're good at, what you like, what's possible, more or less depending on your personality type. And I have a personality type that tends to keep options open."

Which had always been all fine and good. At 27 she found herself craving just a bit more stability in her life. It might be nice to stay in one apartment for more than six months, she figured. It might be a good thing to find a job that paid her enough to make rent and car insurance for once. For Garton, the idea of getting older was a definite plus.

"I've been looking forward to this for the last couple of years," said Garton, who turned 30 in 1997. "Thirty for me has always meant that something would be jelled. Not that a magical thing would happen and that I'd turn around and see everything differently, but that there would be a gradual shift. I've known that there'd be some period of work, work at defining priorities, or really getting to 'The Work.'"

And what, after all that traveling and doing various and sundry things to make a buck, was "The Work"? It wasn't teaching. That much she knew.

"I've been getting this signal for quite a while that teaching is not it," she says. "And now, with this age, turning 30, I'm very interested in pursuing what *is* it." As she leaned toward work in theater and dance, she knew she still needed a day job. Since she never learned how to type ("And I sense waitressing would lead to disaster"), she had to be creative. She wanted a regular schedule but not a rigid 40-hour-a-week gig. She didn't need boatloads of money, but enough to make the rent comfortably every month sans scramble. She wasn't going to kick health benefits or paid vacation out of bed either.

"If my income-making part of my life was not going to be the fulfilling, important work in my life, I needed to get the income work to not be such a struggle," she says. "It was so up and down with the teaching. Whole week periods with no teaching at all. No health benefits, holidays not paid. I was tired of keeping my hundreds of options open and living on the survival edge all the time."

So she found a part-time gig with Kaiser Permanente, as a neuropsychological tester. Sounds, ah, interesting. "It is," she assures us. Now she spends her afternoons evaluating patients through a specific series of questions before they see their doctors. It pays the rent with no problem, and she gets to meet all sorts of interesting people. In the meantime, she still teaches English to Russian emigrees a few days a week and pursues her interest in dance and theater. "It's a good thing I turned 30," she says. "It means I get to have goals."

Fear of Growing Old

Geezerhood for us is another concept entirely. When you ask most women how they honestly feel about growing truly old, many will admit to intrigue. "I want to be a wrinkly, wild old woman with amazing stories and enough strength left in my arthritic hands to get in a decent grope every now and then," declares Drue Miller, 31, a writer and designer for the World Wide Web. Somebody shout Amen.

Getting old isn't as hair-raising (yet) as the idea of growing up. Growing up is more immediate, something we should start thinking about doing any day now. But turning 65 is farther away from us than turning 30 ever was, which means it looks pretty implausible from where we stand. I would caution you to remember how at 20 the age of 30 seemed like the distant future, and look how fast those 10 years went. You might already be noticing that a year now has the feel of a longish Thanksgiving vacation. Put these two facts together and project forward into the future. (As if you can even imagine yourself with children yet, much less grandchildren.) On getting really old, I should think a chick would consider herself lucky to make it that far. A hundred years ago, if a girl made it past childhood and then survived childbearing, she'd often live well into her 70s or even her 80s. Even today we can expect to out-live men by at least a good decade (and if that's not something to look forward to, I don't know what is). As long as they fig-ure out how to cure Alzheimer's disease before I hit 60, I say bring on my dentures!

Every chick has (or should have) a grandmother or an aunt or a cousin they can point to as their old-age model. Some women start playing bingo, but some women start taking tango lessons. On Nile cruises. With scandalously younger men. Some women wear their gray hair and wrinkles with the pride that goes with a life fully lived. These women age with so much power and grace that you start to believe in the wisewomen legends. They don't care what the magazines say, and laugh off everything Hollywood dictates about old women. They'll evap-orate the brain of any man who utters platitudes like, "I bet you were attractive in your youth." While their elderly male counterparts are now crying over what to do with themselves in retirement, these women are launching political lobbies, organizing community volunteers, and helping raise their grandchildren. My grandmother, God bless her, used to insist that she was still 18 on the inside, damn it, it was her body that went soft on her. "Now pour me another beer, darlin' . . ."

Gloria Steinem once said that women are the only group that becomes more radical as they age. When you look at it like this, I don't see any reason not to get an early start.

Fear of Losing Gen-X Clout

Let me just point out that the term *Generation X* was coined way back in 1992 by Doug Coupland (who is now dangerously deep in his 30s) and was, I'd like to hope, never meant to be the all-purpose marketing tool it's become. It's since been used to describe everyone from 18 to 29 years old as either a brilliant, self-reliant entrepreneur or a sullen slacker. Wherever you fall on this consumer spectrum you have to admit that all this ink on our behalf is kind of nice. It's like being in the popular clique for once. Which is precisely why we don't want to lose it. Just as those boomers can't stand the thought of themselves as frumpy middle-aged types, we don't like phasing out of the hip demographic.

When we hit 30, nobody is going to want to know what kind of music we listen to anymore. Nobody is going to ask us to rate a new kind of potato chip or ask us what kind of sneaker we're more likely to wear. And you know what? We know it, and *they* know it, those X-ers, safe in their early 20s. And they're being damn smug about it, too, little beeper-wearing bastards.

"You might think you're still down and hip with what the college kids are doing," says one chick I know. "But you're not. And they're looking at you like, 'God, she's 30, why is she hanging around us?'"

Think about it. Don't you remember what you used to think about the poor wretches turning 30 back when you were 22, not so very long ago? Thirty seemed pretty old, didn't it? You judged those losers who were still hanging out with you at 30 pretty harshly—never thinking that one day you'd be there yourself—didn't you?

Of course you did. That's another reason turning 30 packs such a wallop. We remember what assholes we were. When I started college I competed with another woman for the attentions of a certain man. This woman was earning her graduate degree in dance from UCLA, and she was in great shape. In fact, she had the kind of smoky-eyed beauty that filled me with insecurities and made me realize that I would lose out to her in this instance unless I played my trump card. She was 30 years old. I was 18.

"I can't believe you'd want to go out with her," I drawled malevolently to the man in question, who was 23. At the time, it was inconceivable to me that any man would choose some old, worn-out woman over me. The really horrible thing is I meant it. Thirty years old wasn't even on my radar yet, and to me, such women should have been off the market years ago.

I can look back on this whole scenario now and picture what she must have thought of me, an 18-year-old snip. I remember the dark twinkle in her eye, the way she mockingly looked me up and down, before calling the boy into her hallway and out of my sight to give him the quick tongue. She was toying with me. I'm quite sure she and I could have been fabulous girlfriends, had my natural youthful prejudice against aging (and misguided interest in a man) not prevented it. Anyway, she let me get the man. And, man, did she have the last laugh.

Lesson? Let the pretty, doe-eyed things hang themselves with their own rope while you smile knowingly in the foreground. They'll learn for themselves soon enough. And then you can all have a good laugh.

Fear That You've Run Out of Time

I really hate to be the one to confirm this, but it's true that when it's 30 time, there's a shift in the way society sees a girl. If you were planning to be one of the beautiful young hotshots of the world and get your picture in *People* magazine, sorry, the statute of limitations is up. No matter how deep your cleavage or how loamy your loin, Hollywood might not even have you, unless you suddenly and convincingly lose five years. At 30, all people over the age of 60 begin to ask you why you're not married, why you don't have a boyfriend, what's wrong with a nice girl like you, are you a lesbian, and do you want to meet their nephew Chuckie.

Yeah it sucks. But there it is. If you don't like it, move to some country where they revere their elders (although in these countries you're likely to be stoned as a witch if you reach 30 without producing children). You really can't win. What you have to do, then, is change your attitude.

"The crisis in your 30s is that you feel your day is upon you, whereas in your 20s, everything was always 'someday,' " says Eugenie Wheeler, a sociologist who writes a weekly newspaper column on aging.

Ask yourself this, though: what the hell did you want to do before you turned 30 that you really can't do after 30? OK, so maybe you can't be a nymphet, but let's get real. Cara Fulton, 31, joined the Peace Corps when she was 29, mostly because the opportunity fell in her lap. She'd started graduate school in adult education, and had the choice between finalizing her course with a stint in the Peace Corps or writing a thesis. "The idea of the Peace Corps had always interested me, and the idea of writing a thesis never had," she says. "I spent my last nine credits in Honduras." Not for a minute did she think she was too old.

"Joining the Peace Corps 'at that age' was great," she says. "I had lots of experience to draw upon to do a really good job, and I amazed myself with how focused I was. The younger folks were having a hard time with everything. The whole experience was a real high point for me."

See? Unless you have tangible responsibilities like children, there's no written rule that says you can't sail the seven seas or do whatever you had in mind. So go on and do it now. You've got nothing to lose except maybe your credit rating.

Fear You're Turning Into a *thirtysomething* Character

thirtysomething was evil. *thirtysomething* was how our lives were *not* going to turn out when we, then secure in our 20s, turned the dreaded three-oh. Its characters seemed self-obsessed, confused about what they wanted, selfish, whiny. They were everything we were afraid of. I remember one episode in which Hope, the mousy main character, almost left her husband and children to take a journalism job in some other city. I would slap hand to forehead and scream at the screen (to my long-suffering boyfriend's constant embarrassment), "If she felt so strongly then *why* did she drop out of the *job market* to have babies in the *first place? Why* would any *moral* person abandon babies for a *job? Why* is she such a *bimbo?*"

Nancy was cold. Michael was slimy and calculating. Shepherd, while certainly a minor god in terms of looks, was just another commitmentphobe dork. The only character I ever liked was Elliot, and he got maligned all over the place. Needless to say I watched *thirtysomething* every week until it was canceled.

Fear of That Ticking Sound

When it comes to fear of aging in this generation, turning-30 angst is pretty much an equal opportunity offender. There are a lot of guys out there who have some pretty high expectations for themselves, careerwise, before they hit this magic age. But only we women get hit with the double whammy. Not only do we feel we need to be running General Motors by the time we're 30, but we're supposed to have had three lovely children by that time as well. If we haven't, then we start hearing certain ancient biological imperatives ticking loudly, even from our seat at the head of the corporate conference table.

"When I was younger, I was one of those women who said, 'I'm never getting married, and I'm *never* having kids,' and I had everyone fooled," says Dawn Wallace, 31, an artist. "Then around 25, I changed my mind. I wanted kids bad. Every month I'd get my period and it was a real bummer."

You can't win with childbearing. If you don't have kids yet, you convince yourself that the jig is up and all those years so selfishly spent at college and travel and career building have surely rendered you infertile by now. When I hit this stage all I could think of was Matt Groening's brilliant "Life in Hell" comic strip—and one cartoon in particular, the one in which the female rabbit stands on a street corner with a sign that reads "I am 30 now and want to have children." That cartoon burned into my brain when I first saw it in my early 20s. "I will never be that rabbit," I vowed. But guess what? I was that rabbit.

"I've always loved children," says Emily Schwartz, 31. "And if someone had told me 10 years ago that by now I wouldn't have a few of my own and a reliable husband to help raise them, it would have depressed the hell out of me. I guess I expected everything to fall into place without any worry or fuss so I never actively tried to get into relationships which might result in family formation."

If you do the math, much as I did when I hit 30 and neither had babies nor even a boyfriend, it can seem pretty depressing. You meet a guy. Wait a suitable two years or so to get married. Wait another suitable amount of time before you bring up the question of children (guys are never in the same hurry here for some reason). Unless you're lucky or just ridiculously fertile, wait another year trying to get pregnant, then another nine months to gestate. The end result? You may be pushing 40 before you're holding your first child. That's depressing.

Ah, yes, but the grass is always greener. There is no dearth of chicks who did the opposite and had their families early, spending their entire 20s wiping strained carrots off the carpet. The idea of turning 30 holds little allure for them either. "Just because I had my sons early doesn't mean that I feel like I've done it all," says Barbara Boyle, 32, currently taking night classes at a local college. "When I turned 30 all I could think of was that I really needed to get a life."

Fear of Becoming Your Parents

This, I'm afraid, is another one of life's cruel little tricks. In adolescence we vow to kill ourselves should we ever find ourselves in our parents' shoes. In our 20s we are often amazed, then aghast, when someone points out that we are just as anal as Dad was when it comes to finding the one parking space closest to the supermarket. By the time we're approaching 30,

Ten Things You Should Have Done (Hopefully) by 30

1. Fallen in love or had one bona fide orgasm (you should know the diff by now, toots)

2. Written at least one thank-you note on your own initiative (not nagged by your mom)

3. Purchased one item from the Good Vibrations catalog

4. Finished your B.A. (or at least finished with the idea of ever finishing your B.A.)

5. Gotten fired

6. Gotten dumped

7. Gotten over getting dumped

8. Come to terms with what your hair will and will not do

9. Become able to open the mayonnaise jar, change a light bulb, change a flat tire, and kill a waterbug—all by yourself

10. Become able to shop for and prepare at least one hot dish that does not involve pasta

I'm sorry to say, most of us are complete miniatures of our parents.

Maybe it's when you catch sight of your reflection in a window and think for a spit second, "Mom?" then realize it couldn't be your mom because she doesn't even know this shoe store exists . . . and then you stop dead in your tracks. That was *you*, honey. Not Mom. It's no good trying to tell yourself it was just the tracksuit you were wearing while doing the laundry, or an atrociously bad hair day, or just a revealing hit of direct sunlight. You're looking more like your mom every day now, aren't you?

Perhaps you're not looking so much like Mom as sounding like her, and I don't know what's worse. "This place is a pigsty!" you bark at your husband, then clap your hand over your mouth when you realize that's what you heard from Mom every time she ventured into your room. "Sorry, sweetheart." Cringe. There it is again. Turning into your parents, I'm afraid, is a nonnegotiable aspect of getting older. Sorry. So sue me. Your parents would.

But it doesn't have to be such a horrible fate. It is possible to do some constructive preplanning en route to becoming an exact replica of your parents. Stay away from those Kmart tracksuits your mom seems partial to, for example. I don't care how hot that blue-light special is. Stay away. Tell yourself that when you are her age, you will weigh 30 pounds less and you will not have more than one dog living at the house at any one time. Begin work on those problem areas now, before the problems become apparent. Avoid the urge to drive a Buick.

Fear of Not Becoming Your Parents

For those of you who butter your croissants on the more traditional conservative side, there is the very rational fear of not being *able* to become your parents. Think about it. You're almost 30. At your age, your folks had a mortgage, three or more well-dressed children, a couple of late-model cars (one of which had to be a blue or tan station wagon), a lawn, and possibly a country club membership. Your mom most certainly wasn't whining about turning 30, being way too busy at the PTA or a women's consciousness-raising rap session. Your dad probably had a job that paid him enough to buy all this stuff himself and support everyone else. It no doubt included a pension and health insurance. He wasn't worried about being downsized or rightsized or otherwise told he was out of a job, and he could afford to take the lot of you on some hellish car journey of a vacation every year.

You, girlfriend, will probably never have any of this. Unless you're a movie producer with an accompanying six-figure salary (and even that won't heft it in some areas of the country), the probability of you ever replicating your parents' middle-class lifestyle is pretty low. Not when the entire social contract they hinted to you as a young child has now been torn up and turned into hamster cage lining. Never mind whether you want such a life or not. For some chicks it's just the damn principle of the thing.

Fear of Everything = Escape!

Fight or flight. In cases of extreme fear, such as turning 30, I'd always recommend flight. A flight to a balmy deserted island with several swarthy young bucks is a good option. But me? I flew to Israel (hoping to meet some swarthy young Israeli fighter pilots). One month after my 30th birthday, I signed up for a three-month volunteer stint on an Israeli kibbutz that would begin in the new year.

"A kibbutz?" gasped one friend, in between bites of her $8 Dean & DeLuca sandwich. "What are you thinking? I did that in college. You'll be the oldest one there by 10 years."

This isn't what I particularly wanted to hear by way of support. "But the brochure says it's for ages 18 to 35," I said. "And I just want to get away from it all for a while and clear my head."

My friend snorted. "Bullshit," she said. "Why would anyone older than 25 go to a kibbutz? You're not going to have anything in common with anyone there. And what about your career?"

I couldn't look my friend in the eye and admit that my career star had gone dwarf and was fizzling out. But she had a point about the age thing. Everybody I'd talked to who'd ever been to a kibbutz had done so in college, or in some cases high school. I could end up feeling a lot older than I actually was if I had to spend my time listening to a bunch of kids cry over their summer homework projects.

Still, the idea of a kibbutz had historical appeal, despite what the reality might be. For one thing, I liked the prospect of performing mindless manual labor so I could clear my head but still be productive. I had a thing about manual labor. Many times in the course of my professional career I'd daydreamed about it. During periods of intense pressure, I'd romanticize the idea of taking up a trade, becoming a journeyman tile-layer or hardwood floor installer, and going out on my own. I could learn a lucrative skill that didn't involve my head at all, just my hands and enough wits to get people to pay me for it. On days when I sat despairing over a deadline staring at a nearly blank screen, I'd think how good it would be to have the kind of job where I didn't have to forcibly extract information from people who didn't want to give it out, and where I could perform my craft competently even when suffering from PMS. My life as a journalist went up and down depending on my assignment—some weeks I would be elated at the end of the day, thanks to an interesting story or some nugget of praise from an editor. Other days I'd have to walk around the block to talk myself out of simply walking away and leaving the state, or stifle tears after turning in a subpar piece of shit to a hostile editor who probably thought I was incompetent anyway and now had the proof. Yes, skilled labor, I fancied, might have been a better career choice for me after all. And think of all the savings on student loans.

Despite the misgivings of most of my friends, I eventually found myself at the Kibbutz Aliya desk, the place where they process everyone who wants to volunteer on a kibbutz or make Aliya, that is, immigrate to Israel. Finding out that such a place even existed was a tribute to my 10 years in journalism. (At least I had that much to show for my life.) Not too surprisingly in this age of marketing, choosing a kibbutz was like selecting a vacation package. Which program did I want? A one-year volunteer stint? A three-month with Hebrew language study? An archeological component? I chose the three-month with language program, called an *Ulpan*, from the glossy brochure, mostly because I thought three months would give me a good start in Israel and serve as a base for later wanderings. And why not learn a little Hebrew while I was there? It would keep my mind sharp after a day of picking oranges. The next session started in January, just three months away. As I numbly wrote out a check for administration fees and whatnot, the kibbutz coordinator gave me a rundown on what I'd need to do before arriving at the kibbutz: have a physical exam, get an AIDS test, gird my loins for demanding physical labor. Now I had a date to look forward to. On January 22, 1995, my Manhattan life would be behind me and I would be sitting on a crate on a collective farm, scrubbing chicken shit off of eggs with a toothbrush. Before dawn.

Before I had time to inquire about discreetly getting my check back, the kibbutz coordinator shook my hand, told me to watch out for Israeli men, and shuffled me off to watch a video about life as a kibbutz volunteer. It featured an English girl who looked to be about 18. She met a guy. She drank a lot of beer. It sounded like a pretty good life to me.

2 DENIAL

(No Real Reason to Read This Chapter)

I never know how much of what I say is true.

Bette Midler

I swore up and down that I wasn't going to be one of those tarty women who lied about their age. When I was a reporter at a local weekly (when I was young enough to actually *want* to be a reporter at a local weekly), I remember going into conniptions every time an older woman refused to give me her actual age. It was part of the basic "Who, What, Why, Where, and How" package that I had to get from everyone I interviewed about anything—their age included. But for reasons I could not fathom at 24, certain women always declined to give me their age, and it made me see spots. "Lady," I'd snarl under my breath, "I *know* you ain't 29, OK? Cut the crap and tell me how old you are." A desire to keep my job prevented me from ever actually saying this to some matron's face. But it cemented my resolve that I—and here I'd pound my chest—would always say my age with forthrightness and vigor. I would never let myself become "a woman of a certain age" or coyly refuse to tell a man my birth date. Of course, I had to keep in mind that my own grandmother, a woman of style and strength, who immigrated to this country in the early '20s from Ireland (and then worked to bring over her parents and every one of her 12 brothers and sisters), cleverly lied about her age for decades without a soul knowing. With a deft alteration to one document, creating a nine out of a one, my grandmother became eight years younger. She remained that way until my mother, going through Grandma's papers after her death, found the incriminating document. Clever woman. I wonder if her husband ever knew.

Now that I'm officially in my mid-30s, I can accurately say that I'm not, in fact, one of those tarty ladies who won't give her age. I usually admit my age when asked directly, and when I'm in a decent mood, and when I've been appropriately fed and caffeinated, and assuming I'm not with a group of college girls. Otherwise I'll admit to giving out that information selectively. Lately, when asked my age, I've been known to ask coyly, "Why? How old do I look?" and if the answer is correct, that is, that I look to be in my mid-20s, then I won't grill the questioner on why he got a hair weave.

Why Deny?

Why the hell not? If people insist on doing double takes every time you utter your real age, why not help keep them from becoming members of the Prozac nation? If society's perception of you changes dramatically between the time you're 27 and the time you're 30 for no logical reason, why not employ the time-tested Vulcan mind-fuck and refuse to admit your age to those who will use it against you? Keep in mind that it's not just waxen-faced Texas socialites who shave a few years off their ages when it suits them. All of us girls have grown up soaking in the message that it's better to be young and dumb than old and wise. This is America, after all. So if you find yourself fudging your age after years of not giving a damn, don't get out the sackcloth just yet. You have society to blame.

That said, society could use a pretty dramatic face-lift itself. What would happen if every single woman stated her real age so matter-of-factly that the asker would have to accept it without reaction or lose face as someone who gave a damn about age? The whole stigma of aging would dull, wouldn't it? I think so, anyway. No chick should be ashamed of her age, since we all know that age really does make a woman stronger and better, and if we all got pissed off enough, we could change the notion that turning 30 is something dreadful, something to be feared. Right? Right on!

Of course, then I wouldn't have anything to write about. Never mind.

Pathetic but Necessary and Sometimes Even Worthwhile

So let me be the first chick to stand up and proclaim that fudging your age because of some misplaced societal credo borders on the incurably pathetic. But as we have seen, even I, in weak moments, have found myself engaged in mental combat over whether to be strong and admit the truth or lie just a little and make everything so much nicer.

The whole time I was traveling, for example, I kept my age discreet, unless somebody made a point of asking. What happened more often is the routine passport swap, wherein everybody, either drunk or very bored, looks at everyone else's passport, noting where they've been, and what they look like in civilian life. That's when I'd get the inevitable, "Wait a minute . . . you're 30??!!" Yes, I'd sigh. I am indeed 30. I would then hear the usual (but welcome) remarks about how I looked 23 and nobody would ever guess that I was 30, and then I'd sense a sea change and all my 20-something travel mates would handle me in a slightly more officious manner. I could then imagine them all looking at me in a strange mixture of awe and pity: "It's fantastic that somebody her age is out here traveling around like that by herself . . . but then why doesn't she have a life at home? Ah, I see, without a husband and children she has to fill her life with something, poor girl. . . ."

Most of my 30th year was spent in denial, blissful denial. It never involved actually lying about my age so much as not acting anywhere near it. This was easy to do because after all I was on a kibbutz in Israel, which, as any volunteer past or present can tell you, is just like an adult summer camp. With no responsibility other than to show up for my factory shift (which did take some doing, seeing as it started at 5 A.M.), my inner child ran amok. With no rent, no bills, no career goals other than to avoid being assigned to work in the dreaded chicken house, I was free to be as childlike as I pleased. I danced at random, sometimes to the Euro-MTV playing in the TV room, sometimes to nothing. I perfected my cartwheels and juggling prowess. I wore my hair in pigtails and misplaced all my makeup, deodorant, and jewelry. I engaged in silly arts-and-crafts projects (it fell to me, of all people, to paint an American flag to adorn the volunteers' tractor for an upcoming harvest festival). After my third week there I decided I'd have to go join the drinking games that the lads from England, New Zealand, and South Africa were always having if I was ever going to assert my youth and ability to go the distance. Not that I ever played more than one or two drinking games in college, and of how either of those games ultimately ended I have no recollection at all. But nobody here had to know anything of that, so I gamely joined up and found, to my secret delight, that my ability to absorb cheap vodka mixed with Tang had greatly increased along with my age. And while I could not hope to go drink for drink with, say, the English footballer from Birmingham, I could hold my own quite nicely against some of the wimpier male kibbutzniks. At any rate, the end result of one of these drinking games was that I seduced my future husband, who had been a decent enough chap to wheel me back to my bungalow in a postal cart and never suspected that American girls could show their appreciation in such, ah, creative ways. To this day, the dear man refuses to hold any of this against me.

The moral of this tale: refusing to act your age keeps your skin soft and supple. It might also lead you to a fruitful romance or at the very least keep your sex life interesting and worthwhile. Full-fledged denial can indeed be the fountain of youth.

Famous Deniers

I knew a few underemployed actresses in my New York days, who would keep their share of the rent paid by fact checking at a wide variety of magazines in town. It was a great gig if you could get it. You could make up to $20 an hour by sitting around poring through reference books tracking down elusive facts that the writers of those articles probably made up in the first place. These very chicks told me matter-of-factly that in their field, slicing five years off your age was a matter of course, as was keeping the gray out of your hair and the fat from your thighs. I remember being astounded to learn that one woman, whom I'd always assumed was my age, was actually 10 years older and hence was nearing 40. "Gawd, you have the body of a 22-year-old!" I stammered, enviously, since I, 10 years her junior, did not have the body of a 22-year-old. "What's your secret? Diet? Genes?" She smiled sexily and tossed her chestnut hair. "Denial," she said. "Convincing, whole-hearted denial. I stopped counting how old I was years ago."

I suppose if there's such a thing as hysterical pregnancy and hysterical blindness, one might be able to convince the body that time has stopped and you are still 24 years old. I suspect, however, that this takes just a touch of actual mental illness to pull off. Otherwise you end up like most women—one day passing a mirror and realizing that you've passed the time in your life when you can wear little black midriff baring things and get away with it.

Except if you're a Hollywood starlet of course. Then you can stay in your mid- to late 20s for years. Traditionally, you'd have lied about your age since your first commercial, and at the very first sighting of 30 you'd immediately begin turning 26 every year for the next five. I mean, we all know Heather Lock-lear's not 29, but how old is she really?

Now, however, the trend seems to be that if you're a successful Hollywood chick you should stand up tall and never lie about your age (assuming there's no proof that you haven't been lying about it for years already). It can make good magazine copy. Julia Roberts made the cover of several magazines when she turned 30, and every article was agush with affirmations about the strength of older women. (If only all of us could stop the presses when we turned 30. If only Isaac Mizrahi would donate a frock for the occasion.) Indeed, whenever any starlet admits to having clicked over her third decade, the interviewers trip all over themselves to praise her for her bravery, for her honesty. As if a 30-year-old is in danger of never getting another good female role again due to her advanced age. Although come to think of it, was Hollywood ever inclined to develop good female roles?

Hell, we ultimately have Hollywood to blame for all this age neurosis anyway. *Logan's Run*, the sci-fi movie in which folks live a Utopian life but are put to death on their 30th birthdays, was cleverly released some time in the '70s, when we were at our most impressionable. When you're 10, you don't necessarily see what's so bad about condemning all 30-year-olds to death.

But they're still at it. Just recently I was forced to compare myself to Agent Dana Sculley on *The X-Files* because I learned, in one dramatic episode concerning clandestine birth records, that she had been born in 1964. Gasp! The same year as me! It was horrible. A gorgeous, well-spoken professional compared to . . . me. For the rest of the season I had to stare at her lipstick and wonder "Why don't my lips look like that?" and berate myself for having neither an advanced medical degree nor a special assignment from the FBI. I have to wonder, also, how any normal 33-year-old chick could not have bonked Fox Mulder by this time. It's just not fair at all.

New Youth

I will never get a face-lift because, for one thing, I've never had the privilege of trading exclusively on my looks. I've nabbed my men through a toxic love blend of surliness, ambition, and *chutzpah* (plus I'm a fabulous kisser). But alas, my face has never and will never launch a thousand ships. Plus I'm irrationally afraid of needles and other weapons of surgery, such as scalpels. So I am reasonably sure that when my jawline (such as it is) goes, it goes for good.

So you'll think it strange, then, when I admit to what I did do in my late 20s: I went on a piercing fixation. Why I can stand to get a small rod pushed through the skin of my eyebrow by a guy in a black leather bodysuit with a bone through his nose and yet faint dead away at the mere mention of a blood test in a doctor's office is just another quirk of character that makes me so special. So yes, I got my left eyebrow pierced the summer I turned 28. This was long after the punks started getting pierced, but way before every teenybopper in New Jersey got their noses or navels done, so I was feeling pretty right-on. This was the year I moved to New York and, if the smoker statistics are to be believed, became one of the truly rare birds who took up smoking as an informed, educated, and consenting adult. It was also the year I started cutting my hair shorter and shorter and began dying it exciting new colors. My mother, on one of my infrequent trips home, regarded me strangely. "Why are you rebelling now" she wanted to know, "instead of at 14 when everyone else did?" At the time, I merely sneered and said nothing, proving to her that I was indeed suffering a second adolescence.

In hindsight, however, it is clear what my trip was. Thirty, as a concept, was turning just a bit too quickly into a reality, and I didn't want to help it any. (As if piercings and a nicotine habit posed any sort of roadblock.) And of course, once I moved to the New York office of *Business Week*, piercings had to go. But before they did, these decorations did in fact help me get past the transvestites in front of at least one fairly trendy downtown club, which meant that I had succeeded in proving to myself that I didn't have to look, feel, or even act anywhere near my age. So there.

This sort of behavior can hit a chick at any time after her official mid-20s checkpoint. Check your local phone book for reputable piercing establishments.

The Grand Façade

There is something that can be called institutional denial—when the field you're in requires the utmost youth and in lieu of that, the utmost appearance of youth. Take ballet, for example. And take Sherri Parks.

Sherri Parks had a bummer 30th birthday. She spent it alone in her apartment, recently released from the hospital for dance-related injuries, miles from her family, unable to share her birthday, much less her age, with any of her fellow dancers at the Indianapolis Ballet Theater. For her, turning 30 wasn't just a matter of wondering what to do next in life, it was a matter of seeing the end of her life—her professional life, that is.

"All dancers are like Mozart," she says. "We all die at 37. Thirty for dancers is like 40 for men. It's that pivotal year. And for dancers, it's as if you're looking at your own death. You've only got a few more years to do everything you've ever wanted to accomplish as a dancer."

To compete in the world of professional ballet, you've got to have an unlikely combination of talent, strength, drive, obsession, and whatever body type the companies want in any particular season. You also better have started training by 8 years old. Many dancers who've got what it takes to go professional often apprentice to larger companies by 15, in part because of the tremendous physical demands placed on them. By 25 a dancer is considered in midcareer—that is, if she's not already too injured to continue. After 30 it's the rare talent who is allowed to continue dancing. After 35 only superstars on the order of Rudolf Nureyev or Dame Margot Fonteyn are indulged by their employers.

So the night Sherri Parks turned 30 she was staring the end of her career in the face. Earlier that year she'd been dropped from an overhead sit lift, landing on her left elbow, dislocating the joint near the shoulder, and shattering her forearm. She had just gotten out of the cast and sling when, rehearsing for a *Nutcracker* production, she was slashed in the eye during a crossover in the Snowflakes scene. Naturally she kept on dancing, ignoring the pain as every good dancer is expected to do, and ended up with a corneal ulcer. Seven days in the hospital under antibiotic therapy couldn't prevent her from losing 50 percent of her vision in the right eye. She had massive headaches and dizziness from trying to focus for turns and balances with only one eye, and this lack of depth perception made her nauseous.

"I was a mess," she says. "I hadn't felt so old since I was 28, when I was so overworked and overtired that I sounded like a 60-year-old every time I got out of bed."

Naturally she'd lied about her age for years. Everybody did. It was a requirement in ballet. "Everybody lied in the company," she says. "My best friend and I told each other everything—except our real ages."

No one wanted to hire an "old" dancer, much less an injured one. Confiding any of these fears to anyone in her company would have been suicide, since that would have been all the ammunition they'd need to fire her and replace her with a newer, less crippled model.

She remembered early in her career, shifting from one sore foot to the other as the director and the ballet mistress of the New York City Ballet dissected her. They really liked her technique, they said. Ditto her body and her style. But they just didn't know if they could offer her an apprenticeship that season because, after all, she was so old. "I was truly over the hill," says Parks. "I was 19."

She should never have admitted her age in the first place. "I learned that being old was possibly the worst thing you could be," she says, "except for the greatest taboo of all—being fat." She squeaked by only because she was very, very thin—97 pounds at 5 foot one. "And they wanted very thin girls that season," she says. ("Darcy Kistler and I weighed the same," she says, remembering the pride she felt then at the fact. "And I know because they weighed us all in front of each other.")

After her apprenticeship, she had learned many lessons. When she auditioned for the Indianapolis Ballet Theater in the spring of 1984, she shaved five years off her age and was snapped up as a soloist.

Funny thing about ballet, says Parks, the hardest part is making it look so easy on stage. The stress, overwork, worry, and starvation routinely make kids in their early 20s look 15 years older. But that doesn't matter. What matters is how a dancer appears on stage—physical, emotional, and mental health be damned.

On her 30th birthday, the physical, emotional, and mental strains of her work were all catching up with her. "I tried to avoid self-pity that evening," she says, "but there I was, 30 years old, realizing my career was possibly over, and I had no money, and no other training. I'd barely made it through high school!" All she'd ever done up to that point was point her toes, she says, and the thought of doing anything else simply never crossed her mind. "Up until now I'd cheated the devil by passing for younger than I was." But now, at 30, she found herself far from home, with no family or friends, and no way of admitting to her real age without losing her contract for the next year. "I was having a full-blown midlife crisis at 30!"

Her despair deepened when she started pondering how to make a living outside of dance. How would she pay for all the physical therapies she knew she would need? If she went to college to learn a skill, how would she pay for it? Where would she live? The obvious outlets for all her years of training and hard work—choreography and teaching—were just as crowded as performing, and just as ill paid.

"I suddenly had great empathy with first wives," she says, "who are unceremoniously dumped out into the 'real' world after working incredibly hard for years and years, uneducated, and with no skills that society values. Since your face and your body are your only value to society, once they start to go there's not much compensation."

She was saved by the arrival of a package—special holiday delivery—from her mother. It was a beautiful dress: antique green with gold lace, wide draped shoulders, and a handkerchief hem. Dangling gold earrings too. And a telegram: "Happy thirtieth. Love, your 50-something mother."

Good old Mom! This development was already making her night a lot more tolerable, less lonely. As she hung up the dress on her one padded hanger, the phone rang. Since nobody in Indy knew her secret and all other calls were from telemarketers, she was shocked when she heard the voice of an old flame on the line.

"Happy 30th, toots," he said, a bit of static on the line from calling over the Blue Ridge Mountains of North Carolina. They talked for hours, catching up on the years since they'd lived together in San Francisco. They'd split up for career reasons—hers. His elderly parents in another state had needed him, and Parks had just gotten a soloist gig with the San Francisco Opera Ballet—not something she was prepared to give up lightly. "But we'd only untied the knot, never cut it," she says. "We kept in contact as I traveled around guest-artisting with different companies."

"As we talked, I realized there was a whole world out there—more than half my life, theoretically—was left to live," she says. "And I realized that the end result of our youth culture was that I never had felt 'young.' I was always racing the clock, always already too old. What a waste! I was only 30. It could be the best of all worlds—old enough to know better, young enough to do it anyway, old enough to know I didn't know jack shit, young enough to keep hoping I could learn."

Her mood immensely improved, she tried on the new dress and snapped a Polaroid of herself in it at an oblique angle in the mirror to send to her mom along with a thank-you letter. She then made plans to go to North Carolina for three weeks—right after *The Nutcracker* was over. Then she went to 7-Eleven, bought some cheap champagne and a Sara Lee chocolate cake, and called the one woman in her company whom she considered a friend.

"Jane," she said, "I want you to come over. It's my birthday . . . I'm 30." She clenched her teeth as she uttered the dreadful number. Jane was 24. The truth was sure to be all over class the next day. But the voice on the other end of the line just laughed.

"I'll be right over, little sister," Jane said, and as if reading Parks's raised eyebrows over her choice of phrases, added, "I'm 31. See you in a bit."

Sitting in a cafe near San Francisco's Castro district, Sherri Parks, at 41, can still easily pass for 10 years younger than she is. From behind she could probably pass for a 10-year-old. She is tiny and certainly weighs under 100 pounds. She has that curious elfin quality trained ballet dancers never seem to lose. She laughs when she thinks about the night of her 30th birthday. "I can't believe I was so worried about it," she says. "I was so young, but I felt so old."

Parks is again at a crossroads. But this time it has nothing to do with age, and everything to do with getting what she wants out of life. After leaving the Indianapolis Ballet Theater, she returned to the San Francisco Bay Area and began dancing with a small regional company, one progressive enough to think her "advanced" age was a boon rather than a disqualifier. "The San Francisco Opera Ballet wouldn't even talk to me," she says, by way of comparison. By 35 she had started taking nondancing jobs; as an apartment manager, as a temp, anything that would pay the rent. Time and inclination to continue her dancing slowly ebbed away. At one point, she realized she had all but stopped going to class. "I stopped dancing almost completely for about three years," she recalls. "But lately I've realized that in order to be happy I have to have the dance in my life in some way—just not the way it was. I can have a complete and full life *and* dance." Earlier this year she began class again, at first taking pains to avoid pro classes where her former peers might see her and comment on her technical decline. "But then I realized that was silly. I don't care what anybody has to say about my technique anymore."

She's come a long way from the days when she would have done anything to have George Balanchine cast an eye toward her during class at the New York City Ballet. Does she miss those early days? Would she ever want to be 22 again? "Oh Jesus, no," she laughs. "There are only a few things I liked about being so young, and one of them was that feeling of invulnerability, feeling like there's still plenty of time for everything to work out right. But aging isn't about putting a bow in your hair and pretending you're 18 when you're 35. The values of youth can be carried with you for life, if that's what you want. You can be young and impulsive and hopeful and still be wise."

After some 10 years back in San Francisco, she's making plans to return to the small town in northern California where she grew up. The hubbub of city life no longer satisfies her, she says. Besides, she's found out there's an old ballet studio in town that's been closed since the last ballet teacher retired. . . .

"I'm finally at the point where I'm thinking about the

future," she says. "My future. Dancers aren't trained to think past the next performance, and I think sometimes it's taken me this long to untrain myself."

Basic Biology

Look. I could spout on anecdotally for years about the various woes of turning 30. But sometimes even I have to lay on a few facts, just to really ram an idea home. Not that you don't already know how your body is starting to feel now that you're reaching the upper echelons of 20—and you're not even a professional body abuser. You've probably been sensing it for a few years now. You've noticed that the tweaked ankle you got waterskiing last month took a lot longer to heal than you remember from your high school days. The optometrist down at the Cheapo Frame shop has just informed you that your prescription needs to be upped and now. He was probably just trying to be helpful when he explained that your eyesight will continue to decline every year after your mid-20s. And he probably chalked up your resulting pained look to gas.

It takes three Advil to accomplish what two used to take care of nicely. You've got aches and pains in suspicious places, and your feet ache when you get home at night. Don't even mention what's happened to your ability to stay up all night ingesting various substances. Sure, you can still pull an all-nighter, a back-to-back if the need really arises. But at what cost? The remainder of the week spent in mental traction? While you can be proud that you can pull this kind of stunt from time to time when your job demands it of you, keep in mind that you used to do this for sport three times a week or more.

The facts, then, bear out your secret fears. You're not as young as you used to be. Your body, which was invincible not five years ago, is now on the wane. Indeed, in the medical community, 30 is the crossover age between growth and decline.

"Now, 30 is really very young, in terms of aging," says Dr. Walter Borz, a geriatrician at the Palo Alto Medical Clinic in Palo Alto, California. "But there's a sort of global consensus that age 30 is when senescence, or the body's natural decline, begins. It's the age when growth factors have played their hand."

Most physiologists agree that in general we don't start the drastic decline until 35—that's when the estrogen levels start to plunge, making it harder to get preggers (usually just when you're finally ready to try). Skin loses its elasticity. Hair starts to thin. If you're particularly intimate with your youthful good looks, now's the time to start saving for that first face-lift. For supermodels, it's all downhill from here (assuming you haven't been replaced by the next 15-year-old from Kansas already).

But the women on the National Beach Volleyball Team wouldn't agree with that. And I wouldn't argue with them, if I were you. In fact, I would never dare to show my flabby white butt anywhere near the court of these bronzed, muscled jocks. The top players of this world-elite team are all in their mid- to late 30s, says Liz Mazacayan, a top-ranked player who competed in the 1988 Seoul Olympic Games. The youngest top player is 29.

"Women are at their peak physically in their early 30s," says Mazacayan, 33. "I am so much more a complete athlete now, so much stronger, so much more fit, so much more in touch with my body, than when I was in my early 20s." She recently saw an old photo in a volleyball magazine of herself and a teammate modeling swimsuits. "I look at that picture and I was so much thinner and smaller," she says. "But I wouldn't trade that look for the power and strength and knowledge I have now as an athlete. Part of me still wants that 23-year-old body, but that's not conducive to my success now. My trainer is the U.S. weight lifting coach. He looks at me and he tells me I need to get stronger and I say, 'Are you kidding? I won't be able to get into my jeans.' He says, if you want this body here in this magazine, I'm not the person you need. It's a weird thing that plays on your feminine side. But most of the women I know in their 30s who're playing the tour agree; they're at the peak of their careers, and nothing else is as important."

Full Body Dunk

Actually Liz Mazacayan had her own bout of denial right around 30. But it wasn't so much the age itself, since she largely ignored it in the rigor of training, competing, and traveling with the tour. It had more to do with a lifelong athlete's assumption that her body wouldn't betray her, no matter what she did to it. But Mazacayan found out the hard way that she couldn't ignore what her body was telling her, and in the process saw that by this time in her life, a little balance was in heavy order.

Seven days before she turned 30 in 1995, Mazacayan underwent reconstructive knee surgery to repair a torn ligament. "I'd had other knee surgeries before but not a major one like this." It was considered a career-threatening injury. It was two days before Christmas. "I'm thinking, God, this is what 30 is all about."

Up until her injury, Mazacayan and her partner had been the number-one women's beach volleyball players in the world. The National Team had been the winningest team for two years, and Mazacayan was enjoying the fame and fortune that accompanied it, finally able to support herself solely as a pro athlete (thanks in part to sponsorships by the likes of Reebok). It was the top of her profession, the fruit of a whole lifetime of sweat and dedication to her sport. All her life she'd been a fierce and gifted athlete, growing up in an athletic family, playing volleyball on the beaches of Santa Monica, attending UCLA on an athletic scholarship, a member of the U.S. Women's Beach Volleyball Team at the 1988 Olympic Games in Seoul. This kind of knee injury was a blow in more ways than one. "I was just thinking, God, why did this happen to me? Everything I've worked for. All I could think of was getting back onto the court."

It typically takes eight to twelve months to recover from that kind of surgery. Too long for Mazacayan's taste. "I was determined to come back when the season started in April," she says. "My doctors weren't happy. But I did it, and I ended up coming back almost four months to the day post-op. By the fifth month I was winning again."

At first she was cocky. She was the one to beat the odds. She was strong, gifted. She could work through anything. Little did she know she was setting herself up for another injury. Eight months after her reconstructive knee surgery, Mazacayan broke her kneecap. "People think a torn anterior cruciate ligament is a career-threatening injury," she says. "I would rehab an ACL any day over a broken kneecap. Talk about career threatening. A broken kneecap is ten times worse."

Struck down the second time, Mazacayan began to suspect that something had to change. "It was almost like somebody up there was trying to tell me something," she says. "Like I was going to be pushed down again and again until I learned something from this. That I was not going to bully my way through something this major." As if for added emphasis, exploratory surgery on her other knee revealed a ligament ready to snap. She'd been compensating on that knee for her more seriously injured one. "I was a time bomb waiting to go off."

It was a huge eye-opener for her. "It was a really different time for me. That whole year was the beginning of a life lesson." It was the first time the need for a balance in her life had ever occurred to her. As an elite athlete, she never stopped to think or feel, she just did. She got out there, she competed, she won. That had been the bottom line, the only line, for so long. Now, she saw, the way she ran her career was the way she ran her life, and things would have to change.

"It was a blessing in disguise," she says. "I had to learn the hard way. I had to pay attention to what my needs are. I was the athlete who was so physical, and I was gifted enough to get away with it. But now it was forcing me to look at the game, and my life, really through emotions and feelings, which I'd never done before. It took me a while to really be grateful for something as gnarly as that," she laughs.

Her first test was making the Olympic trials. To rehab her injuries and be in shape enough to place would require a full shot of her old self—sheer physicality and obsession. "But this time I stopped and asked myself, how important is this versus my long-term health?" she says. "It was a big deal for me at the time."

She did make the trials, and played, she says, at about 60 percent of her capacity. "I was one game away from making the final four. I did my best." After that she took eight months off to rest and rehab and get herself back up to 100 percent.

In July 1997 she won her first tournament since being injured two years earlier. But it was a different kind of victory. "It's been a long road back, and it's almost to the point where I think I can do this. I can be 100 percent again, but I will never be the same player," she says. "I'm better now because I can't rely so much on the physical. I have to be wiser and smarter in the game, I have to pretty much learn a whole different game in a whole different style that I'm not used to. Actually, that goes for my life, too. I think I've started into a whole new phase."

Temperance? For elite athletes, or anyone at the top of their profession, being hard-core, obsessed, over the top, is the name of the game. It's what makes them successful, determined to continue on long after the rest of us slobs have hung it up and gone home. It's true in athletes and in entrepreneurs. "When we were the winningest team, there was so much pressure," she says. "There was so much stress. I was so high-strung. I was sick all the time and run into the ground. I can look back on that time and see that sure, I had fun, but not as much fun as I could have had."

Her ongoing life lesson, she says, has "taught me to slow down, enjoy the process and not the result. That's been the biggest lesson for me. You've got to enjoy what you're doing, and the process. It's not about grind, grind, grind just so you can get the result."

Mazacayan is coupled now with a new volleyball partner, a

rookie she originally coached at UCLA. So far the woman has broken all of her sport's rookie records, such as winning her third game. "You don't just win in your first season," says Mazacayan. "It's just the beginning. Even in my career, I still think I have a lot more to go. This is going to be my first off-season healthy. I'm not going to be having to rehab. I'm not starting with a deficit. I'm going to start off where everyone else is starting in the off-season."

It had been a startling season. Winning her first game after two years of injury and rehab, Mazacayan saw her new frame of mind clearly. After the win came the familiar rush of victory, only this time, for the first time, it was quickly followed by "Is that all there is?"

"It was the strangest feeling," says Mazacayan. "I think it's because so many other things in life are more important to me now than just winning. Before, that was all there was to life. It was the ultimate. That was what my whole self-worth was wrapped up in, winning and losing. And so when I finally won a month ago, it was like I'm ready for a whole new level of growth. But I had to get to that spot, to win, to realize that that isn't what it's all about."

This new balance extends to the rest of her life as well. She thinks about what she'll do after her career on the court; she's aiming for broadcast commentary. In her personal life, she's more interested in what kind of husband or father a boyfriend might make in the future than she's ever been before. "I mean, I want to meet their parents," she laughs. She's not worried about having kids yet, she says, since she wants to enjoy her newfound perspective before putting away her sunblock for good, but she says she has the same dreams as a lot of chicks:

taking a few years off to raise her children when she does have them.

She's putting what she's learned into her personal life as well. "I've not only learned it in the last few years, but I can apply it. I think most people understand that concept, they just don't know how to apply it. I've begun to do that, and I feel so much happier. It would never have happened if I hadn't gone through all that when I was 30."

The Biological Clock—Fact or Fiction?

Say what you will, ladies. But there's no denying the clock. You can convince yourself that there's still plenty of time to make it in your career, meet the man or woman of your dreams, climb Everest, whatever. But your body is telling you now that it's not going to wait very much longer for that other big-ticket item on your To Do in Life list: babies.

I'm aware of the miracles of science, thank you. I read with great interest the news of the 60-year-old mother and the surrounding controversy. I also read the resulting backlash to said controversy, column after column of women asking "If a man can have children at 77, why can't a woman have one at 60?"

Let me point out the obvious here to all chicks who are now or one day aspire to become mothers: men don't *have* children. They can, unfortunately, *have* young women who will have children for them. Childbearing and child raising are inherently unfair. I don't care how involved or loving a father is, apart from one quick spurt and several months of interrupted sleep nine months or so later, men have little to do compared to women. Nature made it this way, don't ask me why. The facts are that, biologically speaking, the younger we are when we get pregnant, the easier it is to get through the whole ordeal (but heeding nature's intention these days means it'll take you a lot longer to finish college). Nature takes away the privilege after a certain age anyway. So when you find yourself staring at children starting in your late 20s, your body is definitely trying to tell you something. And what it's probably saying is that, career or not, chasing vomit-strewn toddlers is not as easy on the back when you're 60 as it would have been when you were 20. Or even 35. Nature would like us to live long enough to get the kids through high school, after all (they'll be back after college anyway).

So hearken unto that biological clock, girlfriends. It's for real. But does this mean you're doomed to linger on the Baby Gap ads for the rest of your life? It does not. As with most things in life, ignore it and it will go away.

When I was 21 or thereabouts I was friends with a woman about 10 years older who gave me valuable insight into the workings of the biological clock. Apart from becoming the beneficiary of her cast-off professional wardrobe, she told me the following: "There will be two periods when you have baby fever," she said. "The first one will be at about 25. The second will be in your early 30s."

This same woman, now in her early 40s, is a financial consultant with great taste, lots of money to cultivate it, and one of the only happy 20-years-and-counting marriages I know of. She doesn't, however, have any kids, and she is perfectly happy with that decision. She has successfully drowned out her biological clock, as if she'd stuffed it under her pillow for another five years of sleep.

At the time I got her advice 10 years ago, I was dead set against children. They would only get in the way of my career, I reasoned. And since my career, journalism, was so hard to break into in the first place, once I was there, I wasn't leaving—especially not for motherhood, something I saw as saccharine and old-fashioned. I believe I wrote a letter to the local newspaper to this effect, so there's a public record of my bent at the time.

I made it through my mid-20s fairly unscathed, although I did find myself staring longer than necessary at small drooling things in strollers. But I was still in that high school mind-set, where pregnancy was *bad*. Something to be avoided at all costs. Never something you actually considered, because, after all, you were a college-bound career chick.

Denial of this kind tends to last late into a chick's 20s, when the first girlfriend gets pregnant on purpose. The reaction to an event like this often goes way off the charts. Several chicks admitted to me that they simply didn't know what to say to their girlfriends who were the first to get knocked up with intent. "But, you're only 28," stammered one, and then realized how stupid that sounded.

One day soon you'll wake up and realize that getting preggers just isn't the radical idea it once was, what with you pushing 30 and all. There would be no loss of face. No shotgun wedding. Hopefully no need for welfare checks.

I didn't wake up to any such realizations for a good long time. The maternal urge stayed from my hormones until I was 28 and my cousin was 27. She got pregnant.

It was a dark and stormy night when I got the news. I was holed up at work, looking out from the 39th floor at an icy, rain-soaked Manhattan. I decided to see if the phones were still working. They were, so I helped myself to my employers' long-distance rates and called my cousin in New Hampshire.

To say that she dropped a bomb with her news would be an appropriate cliché in this instance, since it left me speechless, nearly blind, and unable to move my small appendages for many minutes. I had never before heard a woman in my age range admit she was pregnant in anything but the most hushed and horrified tones. The way she so casually announced it made me think I'd misheard her. "You're stagnant?" I said, confused. "Well, yeah, aren't we all . . ."

"No, I'm pregnant."

I said nothing. Surely she was joking. I waited a few seconds for the punch line, but none came. Did this mean she was serious?

"You're pregnant."

"Yes!"

"You're pregnant."

"Yes! Isn't that exciting?!"

The Titans did battle in my head. When I regained the ability to speak, I asked if her current state was a good thing. "Oh yes," she chirped. "We've been trying for about a year."

We've been trying? What was this new language, this *patois* of married coupledom? It was foreign to everything I knew. It smacked of responsibility. Of homes owned, not rented, and of sensible late-model cars. The notion of being confident and grown-up enough to *intentionally* start a family filled me with terror. At 28, I was only dimly aware that all over the world, women my age had complete families of their own. And it was considered good and right and natural. But whenever I thought of this I'd shake it roughly out of my head. This was me I was talking about here, after all. Grown-ups got married and pregnant! How could I or anyone I knew have children when most of us still sat at the kids' table when we went home for Thanksgiving? *We* were still the children!

But once again, time had moved on, it seemed, without me. Here again, I realized, my denial had been complete. I had repressed the idea of reproduction, convincing myself that I would never be old enough to get pregnant intentionally, and yet, clearly here was somebody in my own age group, my own socioeconomic background, sounding very convincingly happy to be preggers.

That's when it started. As I listened to my cousin gush on about "the life growing inside me" and detail the list of organic nuts and twigs she was now consuming to "keep my child healthy," it occurred to me for the first time that I would love to be in her shoes. She was at home with the man of her dreams, a man who adored her, and they were probably discussing names, or decorating their nursery. She was sure of what lay ahead of her. She was part of a family. I was at work late on a cold night, postponing the subway trip home because there was nobody there and nothing to look forward to except a dinner of Cheerios (assuming I had milk), and there weren't even any phone messages (I'd checked). My family was 3,000 miles away in California, doing God knew what but I wasn't there to even sneer at it. It was the first time the glamorous Manhattan career thing started slipping for me. That night, I did what any single chick in her late 20s would do in this situation. I ran downstairs for another pack of Marlboro Lights and called Mom to cry.

Of my newfound sentiments, I dared not utter a word to any of my girlfriends, hard-core career chicks all. They'd see me as weak, a failure, unable to go the distance. After all, nobody comes to New York to live a nice comfy life and raise a happy little family. We were black-clad urban warriors, the smart, independent chicks of the *fin de siecle*. We were educated, ambitious, driven, and really pissed off about the wage gap. Breeding was never in our vocabulary. We'd spent our 20s getting to where we were, and we weren't about to stop. Slowing down our important lives to have kids was an abstract idea, something older women did but not us. It wasn't something we allowed ourselves to think about. Even the married ones among us would recoil in horror whenever asked about future children. "Kids?" they'd gasp. "God, not yet!"

But it was late one night, in a bar during one of our girls'-night-out gatherings, over pints of gourmet wheat beer and Patsy Cline on the jukebox, that I was to learn differently. Apparently, I was not alone with my dark secret.

Sarah was the first to bring it near the surface. "I just got a photo of my sister's new baby," she said between quick drags on her cigarette. "Who wants to see it?" She pulled it out of her wallet before any of us could answer. There was her sister, flanked by her husband, holding a small squishy thing wrapped in a pink and white blanket. "Awww," we recited, knowing what was expected of us.

Then she grew serious. Lowering her voice, she asked the question of the moment: "Does everyone here want kids?" she inquired, surveying our faces. Of course, was the general answer. "When?" This stumped us. Asking a group of recent college grads "when" they wanted to have children would have produced the typical answer of "in my late 20s." Asking a group of chicks in their late 20s that same question produces pained looks and increased nicotine intake. How could we answer this and save face?

I spoke first. This is because, as a native Californian, I can not help but participate in group enlightenment sessions and was still unable to stop smiling at strangers after three years in New York. "I'd have one now if I could." The others stared. I'd spoken the unspeakable.

I shrugged. "I would. It's true. I'm ready."

I'd opened the floodgate. Sarah fondled the photo of her niece. "God, so am I," she said. "I am so ready."

"Me too," agreed another. Everyone, in fact, agreed. Not a one of us would have any qualms about possibly putting our careers on hold to wallow in maternity leave. From this truth suddenly sprung truths about our jobs that we'd only just realized as well. But that's fodder for another chapter.

Living at Home—Utter Denial

I'm just not going to try and justify this phenomenon to our older brethren and sistren anymore, damn it. No longer will I apologize for the state of my generation, or for our McJobs with no benefits and a six-figure student loan to pay off that oftentimes downsizes us right back into the familial home. It's not what we want, understand, it's just that sometimes it can't be helped.

That's why I say if you're prepared to get hard core on this issue of denial, then why not move right back home? It's en vogue, after all. The Census Bureau reports there are some five million men and women aged 25 to 34 living back with Mom or Dad or some combination of the two. Living at home auto-

Reality Bites

Five miserable rules to live by if you must live at home.

+ Rule 1: The Prime Objective of moving back home is to Move Back Out As Soon As Possible (MBOASAP).

+ Rule 2: Never get too comfortable. This is the kiss of death for any independent gal. I don't care how well you get along with Mom or how much you like her giant 60-inch color TV or soaking in her Jacuzzi-style bathtub, her life is not yours. Refer back to Rule 1.

+ Rule 3: Aloofness is next to godliness. You've lived with roommates long enough, right? Conduct yourself similarly here. Buy your own food. Pay your part of the phone bill, make your own bed, and don't leave your shaved leg stubbles ringing the bathtub. Keep to your room or your own affairs as much as possible and for God's sake make sure you have your own car. Borrowing my stepdad's Buick almost broke

matically takes care of several of your fears about growing up (*all* of them, to be exact), and if you're willing to swallow a little of that hot and salty pride, you can retain your Gen-X status years after everyone else bit the bullet and got a real life.

If this is the case, go on ahead and take advantage of your parents' better financial state and their desire to help you out. As a chick in complete denial, you get to disavow every vestige of maturity you've gleaned from life so far, and you'll be able to mooch from Mom or Dad with a free conscience. Mom will do up my mom's marriage. Conducting yourself in this way ensures that you won't violate rules #1 and 2.

✦ Rule 4: Limit affairs with local boys. No matter how cool your parents are, while you live with them don't flaunt the fact that you are a grown woman just entering her sexual peak. You will not win points by sleeping away from home for weeks, or for enjoying your double orgasms for the whole household to hear. Living a more chaste life than you're used to will also keep Rule 1 frustratingly top of mind. And no falling in love with the local flora and fauna, either. Remember, you left home for a reason.

✦ Rule 5: Get a job. Any job. And fast. And bank that damn paycheck, girlie-girl, however meager it is. How else are you going to get back on your feet and get the hell out of the bedroom you grew up in? You like sleeping in a room with an Adam Ant poster over the bed?

your laundry and cook your meals. Dad will fix your car. Both will lend you money. You'll be a slacker in every sense of the word, and nobody would ever guess that you're actually 30 or older unless you confirm it with a picture ID, which is just too unthinkable. (Less so for guys, however, some of whom have no problem living at home forever.) Although in theory I like the audacity of this idea, it leaves a lot to be desired as a practical matter.

More likely, the chick returning home to live will be doing

it under duress, forced into the situation by financial, emotional, or physical reasons—and God forbid sometimes all three at once. This is another matter entirely, which demands a totally different approach.

You will have to come down from that giddying high of autonomy you've enjoyed since moving out for college, and return, hat in hand, to humbly ask for help. There will be many humps to overcome in the future, and rest assured, once back with Mommy and Daddy, they won't be the kind of humps you're used to.

Pride, however, will be the first and hardest hump to get over in moving back home. You'll spend a good week or two with your head in your hands moaning over how unfair life is to force you back to the womb when you're almost 30 years old. You'll wake up in the middle of the night thinking "If I can just get one more credit card, I might be able to keep my apartment until I find another job and not have to move home. . . ." You'll draw up elaborate lists of things you can live without in order to maintain your independence from Mom and Dad at this late date. When you start wondering how a girl goes about applying for food stamps, it's time to accept your fate and go.

Your parents might put up a fight. They might lay upon you that chestnut of when they were your age, they were married and had children and a house and two cars and what's wrong with you kids today anyway? You will stare at them bitterly and say nothing, already falling into a surly faux-adolescence common to the adult gal forced to move home. But you need to stay in their good graces, just long enough to get on your feet again. So suck it up for now. (In the ideal scenario, your parents, like mine when I moved back home for six months after traveling and ditching New York, won't be able to believe their good luck and will have the guest room made up for you.)

My folks had made no secret of wanting me to come back to California when I first left for New York. During the winter of '94, one of the worst of the century, my dad made a point of calling me every week to inquire which ice storm we were currently enjoying. The 15th? The 19th? "Here in Ventura," he'd chirp, "we've got 75-degree weather and some nice Santa Ana winds." This was in February. "It won't work, Daddio," I'd yell into the phone. "I'm not moving back."

This is one instance in which my parents proved wiser than I. Actually, come to think of it, they were right about most things as I was growing up too, including acne and boyfriends. They were not only pleased with my decision to return to California, they had reason to be smug about it. I had the option of living with either of them, no questions asked.

I learned, however, that there is no such thing as free rent. There are rules that must be played by, if one is going to survive living at home. You must memorize the rules, and deviate not, lest you find yourself many years hence crocheting afghans with your elderly mother.

3 BARGAINING

Let's Make a Deal

Don't dream it, Be it.

Dr. Frank N. Furter

Kicking and screaming won't help. Holding your breath won't either. Straight-up, abject denial will get you nowhere except maybe committed, and no matter where you are in your life when you turn 30, Bellvue is probably a step backward.

You've tried to deny. But the weeks continue to blur together and the months seem like three-day weekends and that date you've circled in black on your calendar is looming large. Alarmingly large. In fact, it's almost here. You're almost 30 years old and the space/time continuum has not paused. No, not even for a moment. Not even for you. You've got to do something. And fast.

But what? *What?*

First, don't panic. Take a deep, cleansing breath. OK.

Grit your teeth. Set your jaw. Now is the time in a gal's life when nothing but grim determination will work. You must be focused. You must be ready for hard work. You must have a sharpened no. 2 pencil and a clean sheet of paper in front of you.

It's time to bargain. It's time to make lists.

We live in a goal-obsessed society (in case you hadn't noticed). Goals and list making go hand in hand. There's so much stuff to do and want that Americans start making lists to help them quantify it all early on. You drew up little Christmas lists almost before you could read. ("A Velvet doll, a Big Wheel, a yellow Panasonic tape recorder.") You probably compiled lists of dream back-to-school clothes over and over again. Then there were the lists of high school electives you'd take if you could, lists of boys you'd kiss (if they would), teachers you'd fire, drugs you'd tried, girls you hated.

Later on there were lists of colleges to apply to, in order, ranking from Yale to Slug State U, lists of possible majors, lists of classes you needed to graduate, lists of boys you'd sleep with, lists of profs you'd sleep with, lists of dream jobs, lists of contacts, lists of interviews won and of thank-you letters sent, lists of ding letters received. Then lists of better places to work than the dog job you currently held, lists of favorite after-work bars, laundry lists, grocery lists, lists breaking down how long it would take you to pay off your Visa, and of course the list featuring the name and last initial (for security purposes) of every guy you ever slept with.

These are the little lists of life. We all need them. Most of us can't get out of bed in the morning without compiling a quick what-I-need-to-do-so-I'm-not-fired-today list in our heads. But there are, of course, the bigger lists o' life, the most important of which is the dreaded Things I Must Do Before I'm 30 list.

If you didn't have a pre-30 list of your own by the time you were out of college then I'm afraid you just weren't too ambitious to start with. Any 22-year-old who didn't assume wild personal success would be hers by the distant age of 30 was probably hoping for a job at the post office all along. Certainly after reading the third or fourth humor article called "10,000 Things You Must Do Before You're 30," you'd start to think that maybe you'd better start a list of your own, if only to keep up with Smith-Joneses. Because underneath all of these smart-ass published lists is the tacit goad: accomplish something before you're 30 or it's too late.

Now that you're staring 30 in the face, this list has you up against the wall. (How's that for a mixed metaphor?) A quick scan will reveal just how few items, if any, you can actually check off this list, and that's bound to put a damper on your party and make you feel worse than really necessary. It's this damn list that will provide hours of dark despair for you from now until whenever you actually turn 30 because it will remind you of certain realities of your day-to-day life such as: "If I can't remember to buy milk on a weekly basis, then how do I expect to get myself a promotion before I'm 30?"

Now, it's a proven fact that one reason a chick is loath to turn 30 is because she hasn't done what she thinks she ought to have done by this time. Setting aside for a moment the idea that having a list of items to achieve before a largely arbitrary age is something one does when one is a callow youth of 17 (but stubbornly clings to until well after 30), such lists only set you up for failure. When you're a foolhardy girl of 18, turning 30 seems like such a remote thing that you feel you're budgeting extravagantly by assuming all your dreams will be met by then. You're also young and dumb enough not to doubt for an instant that all your plans will come through, that no roadblocks will come up, that no change of plans will occur to you and that you won't fall in love and chuck everything to follow your lover to Des Moines.

By now, however, you may have noticed that life does all it can to remain uncooperative, and that the more desperately you cling to your predetermined schedule, the more likely you are to be abysmally off track.

Try and follow me here. I had a boyfriend who had a younger sister who herself had a girlfriend. We all met one night to take in a flick, but we swung past my apartment first. The girl I didn't know was not yet out of college, but she was quite confident she had her life sewed up. Irritatingly so. Her plan was to graduate, get a job on Wall Street, work there for two years, return to graduate school for an MBA (in a top 10 program, natch), return to Wall Street, make a ton of money, get married, have two children (a boy and a girl, boy first), then start her own brokerage. She planned on being very rich by the time she was 30. Since she was such an arrogant little shit, humorless and with a haircut way too stern for her age, I decided against trying to counsel her about the number of variables in her life plan. I thought it would be best to keep my advanced knowledge of the way things really work to myself, and stay anonymously on the sidelines, where I could applaud loudly as she fell on her face for the first of many times.

I learned later that her plan had quickly gone awry after she'd gotten a job with a bank that was then bought by another bank that promptly made her division redundant. Whoops. That would set her back a good year, and I don't think she had any Plan B to fall back on. I'd say the odds are 12 to 7 she gets to 30 before she's ready to get her MBA. I wonder how she'll take it.

What girlie-girls like this don't realize is that having a list is all peaches and cream, as long as you remember that life usually gets in the way.

You can also, statistically speaking, generally only get to one or two matters on your list and do them well anyway. This is the nature of the list. It's all about patiently waiting and doggedly pursuing, and most chicks in the universe are deliriously happy if they can cross off even one big-ticket item before beginning their third decade. If you are one of those rare women who can hold up her list and snottily point out that you have, in fact, accomplished all you said you would by 30, then you probably didn't have a very imaginative list to begin with.

However, lists, while inherently flawed, are still a necessary tool for the girl about to turn 30. Lists, after all, have helped millions just like you focus on what they need to do next for maximum happiness: be it buy new underwear, clean the oven, or break into middle management. A list can show you, in glaring black and white, what your objectives really are.

Got your old list out? Study it carefully. Now pick the one item on it that has the most likelihood of being pulled off ere 30 and get started.

Naked Determination

Think back on all the times in the last 15 years when you wanted something so badly you were willing to go to unprintable lengths to get it. Maybe you were the geek who made the first cut for the twirling flags team in high school, then practiced your triple loop catch until your palms bled because you were determined to beat the odds and make the team (of course you didn't, because you weren't one of the popular girls, but the judges were damn impressed anyway). Or perhaps it was getting that first job out of college—competing with the 557 other people in your major for the two available entry-level jobs in town. If you had what it took then, you've got what it takes now. So grit those teeth, girl.

It truly doesn't matter what's on that list unless it's something ridiculously unreal like being the first chick to colonize Saturn (and even then, hey, I say go for it). What matters is your resolve. Keep the following firmly in mind as well: if you're dissatisfied with the merchandise of life at the moment, now's as good a time as ever to do something about it. Exchange it for different merchandise. Exchange it for cash. Decide you don't want to buy anything after all. Burn down the store. You have scads of options. Because remember, you also have a whole decade before you're 40 to set things right.

The items on your list may vary slightly. Even if they do, the trick of working from a list is this: broaden, broaden, broaden. Almost anything is doable if you broaden the perimeters enough.

Start by picking the one item that will give you the most happiness. Say this involves navigating the Mediterranean with the Greek chaps. Let go of a few details and you might be able to pull this one off. Try getting to Greece first. How about your next vacation? Then book a cruise. Lots of Greek sailors on cruises since they're needed to run the boat. (And if you're an American chick you're almost guaranteed to attract several Greek males interested in learning more about, um, your country.) You can buy olive oil and figs once you're there.

Now that's not too hard, is it?

Things You'll Have Done by 30

Let's look at a representative sampling of items typically on a pre-30 to-do list, shall we? The average list includes the following general wants:

✦ Marriage to a handsome, funny, dark-haired man about three years older than you who is an associate professor (tenure track) at a respectable midsize college in an appealing university town.

✦ Babies. Three of them. Brilliantly spaced. Well behaved. Gifted. Named Arielle, Scott, and Jason.

✦ Your name in the *New York Times* at least once, preferably in an article written exclusively about you and your brilliant career/start-up/new play/installation/sculpture. (But a wedding announcement will do.)

✦ Navigate the Mediterranean on a 100-foot schooner with three glistening Greek men and enough pure olive oil and figs for three months.

Try a harder one. You always thought you'd be married by 30 but here you are 29 and boyfriend-free. Not the end of the world at all. First, insist that "married by 30" really means "married between 30 and 35" and *voilà!* Five more years to work with. Secondly, get serious about looking for a serious mate. Consider investing in one of those matchmaker services, because although it's still a shot in the dark, at least you will be set up with men who want to get married as well. Thirdly, stop dating all the dorks who swear they're not ready for the ball and chain until the end of the century and date the ones who still exhibit the natural male reticence but don't protest so much. Since more than 90 percent of Americans marry at least once in their lives (and lots of them do it more), the odds are in your favor that if you want to get married, you'll get married. Insisting on tenure track narrows the field too much because nobody gets tenure anymore.

Are you starting to see where I'm going with this, ladies?

Look, I hate those self-help books and empowerment seminars just as much as you do. But some of my dad's EST training had to rub off on one of us kids, and it seems to have been me, because I really believe you hold the power to change your own life. I know I sound like a TV evangelist here, but bear with me.

Queen of Lists

I was the queen of list making. I mapped and remapped my exact curriculum for each year of college, complete with summer internships and work thrown in as wild cards. I charted my estimated career ascension, and listed and rated cities I might want to live in one day. But it wasn't until soon after my 29th birthday that I drew up the big picture—my own pre-30 to-do list.

A task like this would require the proper equipment: not only a color printer but a nice graphics program as well. So I snuck into work one dark Sunday afternoon to put it all on paper. Lots of women make lists, especially 29-year-old women, but I didn't know this at the time, and so I felt extremely furtive as I drew up my little contribution, then put it into a pie-chart graphic and hit the print button.

Naturally my printer settings were off and I had to break a track record in my mad scramble to find which printer it in fact went to, praying it hadn't gone to the editor's personal printer, behind his locked door, for him to find first thing Monday morning.

My list included items impossible to achieve given the time allotment, as well as things I stood some chance to accomplish if I got aggressive and had a good wind at my back: write bigger, more substantial stories at work; get promoted to the next level on the masthead; make a real salary; get a real apartment; write some fiction; get that fiction published; take time off to travel; meet my husband; have a baby.

Yeah, right.

You can imagine the egg on my face should anybody find such a list. Especially anyone older than 30. Especially anyone male. Especially any older males who happened to employ me in the belief that I was a fully functioning member of the adult race.

I stopped making lists to print out at work when I found my life pie chart on the printer outside the office of one of the magazine's star reporters, a woman in her mid-20s, married (of course), who just that week had detailed her plans to buy a house in the country to a surrounding group of adult editors and little old me, left scratching my head wondering how was it she could think about buying country homes when I couldn't even pay off my Visa. I started making lists instead in my jour-

Helpful Lists for the Girl of 30

We love lists, don't we? They give us order in a world of chaos. They make us feel all snug and secure, as if everything has a chance of working out OK after all. If you've never made a list before (I've never met a chick who hasn't), try some of these time-tested lists and see if they don't put your frazzled mind at ease. You might suddenly feel so together that you run out and balance your checkbook.

✦ Five hot meals you can cook at home in one serving (keeps the Cheerio consumption down and preserves the illusion of a life)

✦ Two male friends who can be called upon for medicinal sex in dire emergencies

✦ The top five Body Shop bath balms

✦ 10 classic novels you'll get around to reading this year (although you've been saying this since college, right?)

nal at home, sitting on my futon and balancing my Cheerios dinner on my lap.

Bargain Basement

But you've always been more pessimistic, you say? You don't buy all that empowerment crap, and with good reason. But

◆ Graduate schools most likely to accept you, in their order of desireability

◆ 15 top reasons to dump your sorry-ass boyfriend

◆ 15 top reasons to get another day job

◆ Five solid reasons you don't need to quit smoking just yet

◆ Everyone you've slept with, in order of appearance, including the chicks you slept with in college

◆ Top five lovers ever, ranked from one to five (hopefully one of these guys is on your medicinal sex list)

◆ Three best Thai food joints in town (that deliver)

◆ Top five thrift-store fashion coups

◆ Top 10 favorite children's names—boys' and girls'

◆ Five classes you plan to take this year through adult continuing ed

◆ Ways you'd spend $100 million in lottery winnings

there's hope for you too, I say. Here's where bargaining comes in. It's a lot more mercenary than empowerment, and, in most cases, works just as well. Besides, once you've gone through the preceding two stages, fear and denial, you're ready to at last take a stab at bargaining. Fill in the following sentence: "If I'm going to be 30 anyway, then I might as well _____."

What did you write? (If you wrote "die," then I suggest you

get your Prozac prescription refilled because there's just no talking to you.) Did you write: "do what I really want"? "shop more"? "get a life"? You're on the right track. At least now you know where the problem areas are and can start figuring out a way to do something about them.

But you really do have to get way more pissed off if you're going to make bargaining work for you. You'll never get anything on your list done if you don't develop a raging, spitting hatred of it.

Let's take my girlfriend Eva for example. When she was 32 she had an interesting job at a place that made CD-ROM games for children, a small but cozy apartment in a university town, and her family nearby but not too close. The problem? No serious boyfriend and whopping debt. "I was so sick of it," she says. "It was way out of control and I couldn't stop myself. I figured if I couldn't have true love then I could at least get out of debt and be a grown-up." Specifically, she wanted to be able to get a loan for a new car to replace the one she'd been driving since her senior year of high school.

To that end, she swallowed her ego and took a desperate step. She signed up with an agency that would manage her personal finances for her. She pays them a percentage of her paycheck directly, and they in turn kindly pay her creditors. Buying new shoes on impulse is a thing of the past, she tells me happily. Her credit cards are all on alert, tracking her spending and ensuring discipline. If she sticks with it, she'll be debt-free within two years and ready to take on a crushing car payment.

Hey, it's a start, right? She got mad, she bargained, she got something done. Sometimes, getting mad is the only way to meet any of your deadlines. Pray that she never finds any really boffo shoes, though.

My Solution

My list was long; my time was not. So I decided to do what I do when faced with an unbelievable amount of work: avoid thinking about it until the last possible minute, cower and pitifully beg for a deadline extension, and then run away from it.

But first, I got really indignant and pissed off.

I had been responsible, gotten educated, worked hard. I had bought right into the career-*uber-alles* idea glamorized in the '80s. Where had such misguided ambition gotten me by my 30th birthday? Heavily in debt to the tune of $15,000 in student loans. A job as an editorial slave in New York City (where what everyone told you when you first moved there was proving all too true: be rich, be a native, or be suicidal within five years). Single and 3,000 miles from my family. The proverbial egg dripped from my face as I slowly began to realize what an insufferable boob I'd been. My life up until then was exactly what I'd made it, and if I had nothing material to show for it, it was just as well. A bigger apartment wouldn't make it any better. The things that were all wrong weren't on the surface. They were in the code.

All the years I spent working late nights and weekends and scheming my next job move, my youngest brother lived my secret fantasy life. He took a few college classes at the local junior college, learned sign painting, then fell in love with an art student and followed her to Holland, where her family was from. He went from one adventure to the next, living in squats, scraping barnacles off of boats for a few guilder, living off fruit and yogurt and cheese. He hitchhiked through Europe, sleeping behind theaters in France when he was short on cash and making it through Yugoslavia just as it was breaking up, trying to make it to Greece before tourist season. My brother didn't give a hoot about college degrees or careers or decent apartments. He had his art, and his friends, and his *chutzpah*, and off he went, seeing the world, to settle when he was good and ready. Damn, but I wanted to be like him.

So in my 29th year, I finally started to do the math. Playing by the rules hadn't led to much. And if at 30 years old I was without material goods to worry about or a committed relationship to nurture, what the hell was I sticking around town for?

What I needed was an alternative plan to the one that was fizzling out before my 30-year-old eyes. A suitable Plan B. After not much thought, I pulled some dusty memory up, one that was unusual, cheap—one that would put me into a decidedly hopping area of the world: an Israeli kibbutz.

Taking the Step

Before you become flushed with tales of bravado like this and begin selling off your possessions, you need to put yourself in the right frame of mind. This means, first and foremost, that you must stop comparing yourself with every chick in the universe.

The Comparing Game

Just as certain mood-enhancing drugs make a girl sensitive to the sunlight, turning 30 will make her ultrasensitive to the accomplishments of everyone else. It is simply a fact of life that no matter how good you are at something, someone out there is better. And if that someone is younger than you, you can bet that the newspapers have already heard about her and have written her up in a glowing article that the cosmos will make sure gets into your hands. You can not be the best, the prettiest, the most talented, at anything. And no, you can not make the best lasagna either. My girlfriend Christina does that. Don't even try.

You'll go through this comparing game again when you're 45, maybe 50, but this one is the doozy. The real shocker. Doesn't matter what you've done to date either. Even the successful chick is prone.

"It's a very personal thing," says Rosemary Ryan, 35, president of Kirshenbaum Bond & Partners, the Madison Avenue ad agency responsible for Wendy the Snapple Lady and other award-winning campaigns. "People deal with it differently. But I think most people have these expectations of what they should have accomplished by that age, and most people feel they've come up short."

This from a gal who was running an ad agency in New York City that had some $200 million in billings when she turned 30. She had helped design a Keds ad campaign that *Time* magazine called one of the best of the year. She had a great apartment. A doting husband. A loving dog. And fabulous piles of red hair. She was the sort of chick who you'd naturally want to hate but couldn't because on top of all this she was extremely likable as well. How, pray tell, does such a chick come up short? Doesn't she already have everything?

"Yes, but you never see it that way, do you?" she says. "It's like Judgment Day. You're forced to really take stock." And, like most of us mere mortals, all she could see was the big, ugly list of what she *hadn't* done, staring her in the face like an accusation.

Even in your own humble peer group, you can't help but compare yourself. There is, in fact, an unwritten scale of where you fall among your own girlfriends on the accomplishments-by-30 continuum that is in wide-scale use, and, if you're smart, you'll make sure it *stays* unwritten. It's for quick mental tallies only. Whenever a new girlfriend enters the fold you simply give her the eyeball, ask a few pertinent questions (these can be profession- and possession-specific) and file her away neatly in the appropriate spot on the scale. Her placement is rated this way: on a scale of 1 to 10, 1 indicating peer in question still lives at home and doesn't date and 10 indicating peer is a highly competent, well-paid professional woman who is married and owns her own condo and is on schedule to be having a baby in the next five years or so. Add one point for manageable hair no matter what other hell the girlfriend is living. Subtract two points if the girlfriend has more than two cats.

Asking around, however, you'll soon find that even the 10s are gloomily picking at their $30 manicure jobs and wondering where they went wrong. "Wasn't I supposed to be a Supreme Court justice by now?" she might ask herself.

She might indeed. But how can you blame a poor girl who has grown up on a heavy media diet of youthful success stories? Starting somewhere in the mid '80s, the media was suddenly besotted with all that glitters and is under 30. It's all around us, this worship of early achievement. Winning the Nobel Peace Prize is all fine and nice when you're 70 and it culminates 50 years of study and hard work. But it makes for a hell of a lot more snappy copy when a 27-year-old wins the prize, don't it? This unfortunate sentiment is echoed everywhere, too, and is almost completely unavoidable. It's in the feature film and the music video. It's in alumni magazines. It's in advertisements. It's probably in the water too.

To wit: I recently flipped through a national news magazine, hoping to bone up on the pop culture and looking for bylines of friends when I came across a full-page ad selling upscale writing pens. The ad showed five pens of increasing style and value, with a time line on top, illustrating the spectacular rise of some hot young executive in the years between college graduation in 1987 and 1996, when this hot young executive takes his company public (and of course we assume it's a he), becomes fabulously wealthy, and gets to retire early. The oh-so-clever twist to the ad copy is that the first humble college graduation ballpoint and the last, gold-plated ink pen are both used by our hot young executive to keep a journal while traveling through Europe. Get it?

All I could see was that graduation date, 1987, which was the exact same year I graduated from college (after being on the five-year plan), ramming home the fact that as of 1996, or 1998 come to think of it, I myself was in no position to be buying $400 pens, thank you very much.

It's not as if I normally spend a lot of time pondering pens. But this ad made me downright petulant about them. Why couldn't I afford $400 pens yet anyway? It wasn't fair. According to this very ad, people my very age were at this moment deciding whether to purchase the blue Du Point Gold Tippe, which got a nice write-up in *Town & Country*, or the platinum-plated Trident III Heat-Seeking Fountain, which matches the new BMW. Clearly, money was being made and luxury items consumed by the masses, but not by me. It left me wondering what exactly was the message meant to be gleaned from this ad. Thank God I never got that internship as an advertising copywriter 10 years ago? Or that I am an utter failure because I am over 30 and still rely on writing implements stolen from work? Most certainly it's the latter.

You must insulate yourself from such media input. This can be difficult, because to avoid hearing about or being forced to look at your more successful peers means you will have to live in a flotation tank (the non-TV variety). But here are some helpful suggestions I've developed to help you accomplish this and still keep your apartment, TV, and *Vanity Fair* subscription.

- Avoid all high school reunions. I am religious about this. Even though I'm almost 100 percent certain that I've had a far more hip and glamorous life than my high school peer group (many of whom live in trailer parks and have almost-grown children), I don't want to pay the 80 bucks, return to my hometown Hilton and find out for certain because it would only lead to survivor guilt. Besides the fact that any and all confidence I've gained after 15 years away from the crap town I grew up in would melt away as soon as I walked through those reunion hall doors. No matter how dark my sunglasses were, no matter how many Gaulois I inhaled and blew impatiently back out my nose, I would instantly revert to Julie Tilsner the geek with glasses, braces, a back brace, and her nose continually buried in a science fiction novel. (Typically, geek girls today enjoy status as the hippest of the hip, but since the personal computer was only just out when I graduated from high school and the World Wide Web didn't exist yet, girls like me were still routinely tripped en route to our lockers . . . but I digress.) And in that state I would sit all evening, looking at portraits of people's children, hearing about the family business, and second-guessing myself about every choice I'd made up to that evening. Unless you were the prom queen, a high school reunion would probably be the same for you. Even if you were the prom queen, everybody would only want to know why you didn't become a network anchorwoman like you'd planned, and you'd leave as bummed out as the rest of us.

- Cancel your subscription to all college alumni magazines. These are no good for your self-esteem at this age either. You will only bemoan those more successful than you (who were complete wankers in college, you recall), or those with children already. Remember my cousin? The one with the L.L. Bean life in New Hampshire? She recently told me how she learned from her alumni magazine that a woman she was competitive with on the college paper was a Pulitzer Prize finalist. The only thing my cousin herself was a finalist for, meanwhile, was the Most Sleep-Deprived Chick Award, as she'd just recently had her second child. "I was depressed for a month," she said.

- Engage in selective information retention. Whenever you hear news of a peer that makes you seethe with jealousy, blot the offending information from your mind immediately. This gets surpassingly easy the more you do it, and you'll find it can be a handy narcotic substitute in many of life's more painful realities. For example, say you're a struggling grade-school teacher who opens the newspaper one morning and reads that some Neanderthal you knew in college who left his credentialing program to go to Hollywood is now making half a million dollars writing *dreck* that passes for entertainment on network TV. You will want to rant and howl about how unfair life is but you will only be wasting your energy. Block it from your mind and focus on better things. Like convincing your girlfriend who works at one of the giant corporations that sponsors his show to send along some corporate letterhead so you can craft some creative complaints that are sure to get noticed by network brass.

Golly, did I just suggest something illegal? Sorry.

- Develop scan-and-avoid skills. Whenever you pick up a newspaper or magazine, quickly scan for ages and avert your eyes from any article with subjects between an age range of 21 and 35. Learn to spot problem word combinations such as "twenty-something" or "brilliant debut" and most certainly anything about "six-figure movie rights." Similarly, when you find yourself face-to-face with the chick who got the promotion instead of you, excuse yourself to the bathroom right away. Tell her it's morning sickness.

Geek Girls Rule

Drue Miller, webmistress, geek girl. One of the cyberyouth now populating San Francisco. Not the sort of chick you'd expect to give a damn about turning 30, except that until she was 26 she was none of the things above—which made her think that as long as she was aging, she might actually have a life before 30.

Drue Miller, a nice middle-class girl born and raised in Pennsylvania, always dreaming of bigger things but never daring to do them. She stayed close to home her whole life, even choosing Carnegie Mellon—the local university—because she wouldn't have to travel too far to get there and she could live at home for free.

Although she was an English major, she fell in with computer geeks because her boyfriend was one and because, well, because she liked computers and she liked geeks. After college she got a sensible job as a graphic designer and moved in with her boyfriend. Their life, she says, was one where they got home from work, watched TV, ate dinner, and got to bed by 11. On the weekends she clipped coupons and went grocery shopping.

Drue and her merry band of computer geeks began to hear reports of the Golden Land of High-Tech—Silicon Valley— the San Francisco Bay Area. "Everyone dreams of moving to California," she says. "You knew that was where you could be anything you wanted to be—any kind of alternative lifestyle you could imagine, there were people out in San Francisco living it." There was a particular lure for those in high-tech as well—the virtual guarantee of exciting and lucrative employ. After several of her friends got jobs out there, she decided to take a chance too. "I realized that at 26 I'd lived my whole life in the town I grew up in," she says. "I thought if I didn't take this chance I might end up staying there forever." She sent 180 résumés into the void.

One caught the eye of an employer, and soon Drue had the means to relocate herself. She, her boyfriend, and a few of the same old friends set up house in Marin County, an upscale suburban area just across the Golden Gate Bridge, where, she says, she replicated her life in Pennsylvania, replete with coupon cutting and nights spent watching the idiot box.

As anyone from the hippie era will tell you, San Francisco has a way of prompting its denizens to push their personal boundaries. Drue Miller knew this. So she didn't question a thing when, for example, she found herself attracted to women for the first time. She just dove in, so to speak, and tasted of the rubyfruit jungle.

Naturally her experiments didn't sit well with the boyfriend. It wasn't long before the two went their separate ways. Or rather, he stayed right where he was, and she went off to find the real Drue.

The Drue she found had torrid affairs with other women. And other men. And flings with gay men. ("Very interesting," she reports.) The job that got her out to California left a lot to be desired, but soon, as is the way in tech circles, something better came along. Thanks to her choice of friends in college, she was never timid around computers or new technology. When she learned about the nascent World Wide Web, she immediately saw what a venue it could provide her graphic design skills and writing talent. One job later, she learned that very big companies would pay a lot of money to people who possessed the secrets of the Web. And so it came to pass that Drue Miller became what is quaintly known in San Francisco as a webmistress.

It's very hard to picture Drue as a nice, clever girl from Pennsylvania. Not when you see her around San Francisco. The first thing you might notice these days are her bodacious biker boots. Or peroxide blond hair. She lives with her boyfriend (straight, yeah, but seven years younger and the mastermind behind the popular webzine *Fray*) and zips around town on her motorcycle with a license plate that screams

"GEEKGRL." There doesn't seem to be much vestige of the girl she left behind in Pennsylvania.

"I think it's kind of natural for women to develop as they get older," she says. "If not better self-esteem, then at least a stronger understanding of who they are. So even though I still have my episodes and whatnot, I don't feel as overwhelmed or as unable to control things. I feel like I can have the kind of life I want now. I can laugh at things easier."

Bargain Enlightenment

I had thought I might be bored, coming from frenzied Manhattan to a sleepy communal farm. Quite the opposite, in fact. Although one volunteer likened life on the kibbutz to "one long, ongoing day," it turned out to be one of those days made to be spent staring happily into the middle distance. There were whole weeks where the most ambitious act I could manage was walking across the kibbutz to the post office to buy stamps. If I had wanted time to detox and think, then I was getting it. With a clear head, no distractions of any kind, I was able to set my whole life out in front of me in outline form. I was 30 years old. I was single. I owned nothing, but I was educated and had certain marketable skills. I was free to go anywhere or do anything I wanted—if I could only figure out what.

The answer didn't come quickly. For a good two months my brain seemed to shut down whenever queried about the big question: what do you want to do with your life? I simply knew I didn't want to be doing what I had been doing. That left everything else under the sun. And what is true about shopping was true in this case as well: I was paralyzed by choices and so

unable to choose anything at all. I kept faithful to the notion
that this time away from my real life would afford me some
kind of perspective, maybe even an epiphany—all I had to do
was keep my mind clear and unhurried. So every day I showed
up for my shift at the factory. I made kibbutznik friends and was
on a friendly nodding basis with the Russian immigrants who
knew no English and were only a little more skilled in Hebrew
than I was. I'd sit with the other volunteers in the communal
dining room for lunch, sipping bad instant coffee and smoking
way too many evil Israeli cigarettes. Every day I'd fight for the
last remaining copy of the *Jerusalem Post*, an English-language
rag with a decidedly right-wing bent, with Luke, an Englishman
who'd already been on the kibbutz for months when I got there.
Every Wednesday the *Post* published the *New York Times
Week in Review*—the only vestige of my former life I actively
maintained, but since some 50 volunteers only got about five
copies of the *Post* every day, it had become something to bargain over. Cigarettes, chocolate, 10 shekels, whatever. Luke and
I struck up a bargain to share whatever copy we could pilfer so
we could argue about the Thomas Friedman columns. Naturally we struck up a fling too. So what if he was six years
younger than I was?

Slowly I let myself give up everything I'd come to believe
about myself. I questioned all the values I'd held, all the goals
I still hoped for. What was I driving for in my ambition that I'd
step all over people I loved to accomplish? Did I covet material
things? Power? Fame? And, if so, what for?

When the truth came to me it was so simple I almost didn't
realize the answer had come at all. I was sitting amongst the
other volunteers, listening to a Brit and an American argue
over a chess game. I loved this—living as part of a community.

I loved waving "*Boker Tov!*" to the old kibbutzniks as I went about my day. Short of living on a commune, how could I import the feeling of belonging somewhere back into my own life? Quite simply, I could move back to California, where my family and oldest friends were. If I loved the city life but didn't fancy living across the country from everyone I loved, why not San Francisco? I wanted a life, and I no longer really equated life with work. After all, I was a writer, right? Why not just write? Why did I have to be on staff somewhere? Of course, experience told me that this way of thinking was a good way to starve, but with just a small adjustment in attitude (growing a stomach for temp work, for example), it could be done.

With this decision made I immediately felt lighter and more focused than I had in a long time. It was like stepping out of the factory every morning at dawn, knowing that the grind was over and that breakfast lay ahead. Suddenly it seemed that my time here was more precious, more limited. Now I had some course to follow, and this free time would end at some point.

I stayed on the kibbutz for nearly six months. It was now nearly July, and Israel had become hot and full of tourists. The group of volunteers I had come to know well had mostly already moved on, and in their place had come what I had feared in the first place—a large group of 18-year-olds. Gone were the chess games, the long group discussions held on somebody's porch, and my feeling of belonging. These kids seemed only to want to party and sleep with each other—which is what we had done too, but we were more subtle about it. Luke had returned to England some two months back. There was no reason to stick around anymore. Anyway, I'd been invited to Cyprus by some scuba divers I'd met on a ferry from Greece. This seemed like a good time to join them.

Cyprus back to Greece. Greece to Turkey. Turkey to Italy, where I met up with Luke again. Italy back to England. All of this on less money than most professionals take home in a month. By the time Luke and I went back to London, scrunched in back of a night bus bound for Brussels, I was pretty much flat broke. We spent a few miserable weeks living on his dole check and trying to stay out of the way of his mum, whose flat we were in. I halfheartedly looked for work in London, but I knew I needed to return to the States and start the process of returning to San Francisco. Much as I loved Luke, I was no longer willing to play the pliant girlfriend, supplanting my own goals for his. I'd made up my mind to return to California, so that's where I was headed, I told him. He could come along if he wanted. As if offering an Englishman a life in California should be considered any kind of a sacrifice.

4 THE COUNTDOWN

The Fat Lady Warms Up

There is no such thing as inner peace.
There is only nervousness and death.

Fran Lebowitz

Ladies, I want you to get out your pens and take notes, because this is the chapter wherein we debunk—or at least kind of explain—the leading accomplishments most often left undone at the time of the 29th year and why, ultimately, you don't need to worry about them yet, even though you're convinced you do. These are the doozies. The ones that never really mattered that much until you reached your late 20s, and particularly after the inaugural 29th birthday (which itself is explored next). That's when you experience a sickening moment of clarity and realize that things are not as you assumed they would be back when you were 19 and the world was your oyster.

29 and Counting

It wasn't exactly the *annus horribilus* the good Queen Liz had, and indeed, had it been any other year but my 29th, I could have shrugged off the entire 12 months and resolved to do better with the next. But it was the 29th, and I guess I expected something to happen. I guess I thought I could pull my life together in one short year so that I could face 30 with something akin to dignity. But this was not to be. Nor was much else.

I had a 29th birthday bash that was nothing short of debauched, in a transparent attempt to show *bonhomie* toward my impending fate. I invited all my girlfriends and every old lover who would still talk to me. I danced on tables, smoked cigars. I abused expensive drugs and reveled in obscene gag gifts. I even commandeered one hapless former beau who fretted about propriety until I got him home to my apartment and commanded him to shut up and service me in a manner befitting a 29-year-old woman. In all, it was a successful night. I had no business allowing even a slightly negative thought to enter my head that night. But there it was, first thing in the morning: "I now have 12 months until I'm 30 years old." Two signs that this was not going to be the year I'd hoped for made themselves known to me immediately: the landlord slipped a note under our door saying that my half of the rent check had bounced; and the former beau had to rush off to meet his girlfriend for brunch.

My hunches were right. My 29th year was not what I had hoped. Work plodded on without so much as a change in job description. I got coffee at the same joint every morning. There was no improvement on the apartment front, and, generally speaking, I got nowhere with the lads.

The summer was particularly bad. The tone was set early on, when I, a girlfriend from work, and her neighbor tried to escape the heat by going to the movies. Everyone else in Manhattan had the same brilliant idea, so we bought tickets for a later show and decided to wait the two hours in a bar next door. The sign outside promised $1 margaritas.

At some point, I don't recall after how many peach margaritas (they were pretty good, and they were only a buck), I began to drink them out of my clog. The very clog I'd had on my foot, although I couldn't say if it was the right or the left foot. At the time this didn't seem gross or even extreme in any way, and my friend's neighbor soon joined in the festivities by using my other clog as a serving vehicle for his margaritas. This went on for about two more rounds, until I was able to vaguely grasp that I was drinking margaritas out of my footwear in the middle of the afternoon. I decided to call it a day. I forgot all about the movie, and indeed barely made it the four blocks home.

Once home, I decided I was in the proper frame of mind to call the boy I'd been pining over, who lived in another state. He picked up. He was just out the door, he said. "Where to?" I gurgled. And ever hopeful, added, "New York?" He chuckled uncomfortably and then decided that tough love was the only way he was going to get rid of me. "No," he said. "I've got a date."

This didn't so much sober me up as turn my stomach. I hung up not to be dramatic or anything but to try and get the two steps from my futon into my bathroom before throwing up in alarming, Day-Glo colors. I half made it, and only doused half of my dress. For the next hour I lay sprawled in the toilet's strong, cold arms and sobbed and puked and sobbed and puked.

I was 29, damn it. Too old to be drinking margaritas out of a clog on a Saturday afternoon. Too old to be playing footsie long distance with assholes who weren't interested. Too old for all of this. I needed a life.

That was the start of my year. It ended on a much worse note. My personal, all-time low came on the very weekend of my 30th birthday, which, as my birthday is wont to do, fell on Labor Day. That summer had indeed shaped up to be the hottest on record for years. And me without a Hamptons share, or a Jersey Shore share, or even any knowledge of how to take the subway out to a beach of any kind. By this time I'd met another guy. One who only lived in New Jersey and not a two-hour plane ride away. He both irritated and amused me in equal parts, but he liked to dine out a lot so I kept going out with him because I could scratch two basic needs at once. It was understood that we were wasting our time with each other in lieu of something better.

One particular sweltering week we decided to get out of the city by any means possible and made a list of out-of-town friends we knew well enough to impose upon. My cousin, the one living in rural New Hampshire, was the overall winning choice, and, with her blessings, we made arrangements to drive up for a visit one weekend very near to my 30th birthday.

In retrospect, this wasn't the most prudent use of my self-esteem. My cousin and I had been as close as sisters when we were young, and hence turned out to be lifelong rivals. She got boobs first; I kissed a boy first. She had the bigger collection of plastic horses. I had the more successful perm. In college, we both studied journalism and wondered whether a Pulitzer Prize looked anything like an Oscar. In our mid-20s our lives careened wildly away from each other and now, God bless her,

I hated her guts because she had everything in life I didn't: husband, home, children, obedient dogs. Her husband wasn't simply some schlub of a man either. He was The Last Good Man. He was kind, hardworking, honest, funny, and handsome. He was also successful with his family business and able to craft entire patios out of stones from old New England fences gracing their eight acres of land. Their home was an old Cape Cod they'd bought and restored over the last several years—a dream of mine in itself—and now it was a paean to taste and class. Filled with antiques, yet comfortable and unostentatious. I had hoped her 10-month-old daughter would fulfill my every stereotype of children by screaming all night and flinging her zwieback on yonder walls. But, maddeningly, the opposite was true. The child was a cherub, cooing and giggling and holding her arms up for me to hold her so often I very nearly started lactating. To top it all off, their three big, hearty dogs were well behaved and stayed out of their garden, where her husband grew large, shiny vegetables for their evening meals.

In short, the weekend was a nightmare of self-loathing and pity. As I slept next to my boyfriend in the guest room (under antique quilts), I broke several commandments by coveting all my own cousin had, hating her for it, and hating myself for the petty fool I'd become. I should have been joyous for her; instead all I could think of was how she could certainly see through my attempt at making my life in Manhattan sound glamorous, and knew very well that I would be returning to a soul-deadening job, a cold room, and an empty message machine.

At the end of the weekend, my cousin handed me a "30 Hurts" pin, a gag gift someone had given her husband, who'd turned 30 the year before. "That doesn't offend you, does it?" she twinkled. She could do that. She had only just turned 29.

And here she had a husband, a baby, a house, and a vegetable garden that grew viable basil.

"Oh, of course not," I lied, while the boyfriend, who himself was 26, looked away. Surely I was the most wretched chick in the universe.

At least I wasn't alone in the wretched chick class. My roommate enjoyed similar status. We were both often between boyfriends, and when one of us had found a bit of love for the month (or however long we could milk it) the other would get surly and snarl in the morning as the lovers emerged, glowing and happy, from the conjugal chamber. During the winter we spent most nights huddled together over a space heater the size of a large box of corn flakes to keep warm, since the heat mysteriously never seemed to make it to the sixth floor. In the mornings we'd crouch in front of the mood-enhancement lamp built by a boyfriend long past, meant to cure seasonal affective disorder and drink cup after cup of life-sustaining coffee. Every Saturday we'd rip open the Style section of the *New York Times* and peruse the marriage announcements, looking for people we knew (and there always seemed to be at least one), and comparing ourselves in looks, breeding, education, career, and, of course, age. We took particular note of all the 33-year-old men marrying 24-year-old women. We promised that when one of us grew old and died, alone and friendless, the other one would alert the proper authorities so that the neighbors would not have to find our rotting bodies in our rent-controlled apartments.

It was during bonding sessions like these that we would invariably begin to sigh heavily and wonder what happened to all that youthful potential we had upon college graduation, and how neither of us had expected to end up like this. Surely, we assured ourselves over and over again, in five years we'd look back on this time and have a good laugh, even though it wasn't terribly funny at the moment.

Recently this friend reminded me of the mantra. "You would say, 'If only I had a crystal ball and could be assured that at some point I'll actually get married and have a baby, I could relax and enjoy being single in New York.'"

Ah yes, I remember that mantra, and the idea behind it, of how it wasn't that I wanted marriage and children right then, but I wanted them someday. And turning 30 without any of it just made me more desperate to be reassured that it would, one day, happen. Since the years were now clicking by at a good clip, all I wanted from the cosmos was some kind of money-back guarantee. It seemed only my due as an American in the late 20th century.

Of course it all did happen, by the by. But, ever the worrier, I was convinced it wouldn't. And so I spent my 29th year in abject misery, going over and over in my mind what I didn't have compared with so-and-so, and creating list after list of accomplishments to nail that year, which I would then lose under the futon and consequently never fulfill. About the only good thing I did that year was start to realize that something had to change, and that only I could change it.

But that kickass inaugural 29th birthday bash helped anyway.

Ten : The Inaugural 29th Birthday

It starts tonight. Better make it a good party. Best if you don't remember details, but if you can, they'd better include all your best girlfriends, expensive and inexpensive spirits mingling freely on a centrally located table, flames old and new. Gag gifts of a sexual nature and a steely resolve to finally get your shit together are always welcome.

Actually, there are several options for one's inaugural 29th birthday. One way is to make sure you squeeze every last ounce of debauchery of the last decade into this one night. Kind of like topping off a full tank of gas. The other is to go into mourning, which, while it takes the appropriate tone for some chicks, makes for a bummer of a party.

I prefer the third option, that of the theme party. If the idea is to launch you into the final year of your 20s, why not explore some of the central ideas that careened through your 20s? I like the idea of a "bad first suit" party, assuming you can still fit into it.

Or how about "the spinsters' ball," replete with bridesmaid's dresses from the last 10 years. (You might as well put them to some use, right?) A theme sure to get lots of yuks is "dead dreams," or the ever popular "wear what you thought you'd be by now" party. Don't forget the liquor and drugs. Never have they been so important.

If your inaugural 29th birthday turned into your own personal lost weekend, remember, it's just the first one. There are as many in your future as you'd like, so you've got plenty of time to perfect your technique.

There are several well-trodden areas of the aging process that you may be particularly sensitive to in your 29th year. I know a chick is apt to be particularly thin-skinned and humorless about these physical markers, but I urge understanding and restraint. Prove your growing maturity by not lunging at your boyfriend when he points out the laugh lines around your

Appropriate Gifts for the Inaugural 29th Birthday

+ A gift subscription to *Modern Maturity*

+ A pirated prescription for Retin-A

+ Designer drugs

+ One-year subscription to the Good Vibrations catalog

+ Dating service membership

mouth. Do not let the fact that the wounds from your last in-line skating accident took almost a month to heal stop you from getting right back in there for more. Have a sense of humor, for God's sake.

Nine: The First Gray Hair

Excuse me, but if you're nearing 30 and have only just *now* discovered your first gray hair, well, you can just kiss my Miss Clairol Medium Auburn Permanent Color. I have little sympathy for you, I whose first gray hair was plucked from my downy head as a lass of 21. I was in the newsroom of my college paper, as I recall, and one of the photographers (it's always one of the photographers) crept up behind me and bellowed as she pulled the errant hair: "Tilsner's got gray hair!" As the jokes commenced, I snarled that somebody at that fish wrap had to do the worrying, right? At this time I was still young enough to think that I was the sort of chick who'd never dye her hair. Sorority sisters dyed their hair. My mom dyed her hair. I did not, thank you, dye my hair.

By the time I was 27 I was dying my hair regularly, mostly (I told myself) to zap up my natural "mouse-shit-brown" color. These days people can see the gray hair through the color, and my roots, God forbid I let them see the light of day, indicate that I will be dying my hair until I'm damn good and ready to look the part of Grandma Tilsner.

But if this discovery is new to you, take heart. Don't look at it as a sure sign of aging. Look at it as, I dunno, a welcome change in hair texture. Besides, I've known several chicks who simply let their gray hairs take over—to fabulous results. One in particular wore her graying blond hair down to her waist, and it looked pretty kickass. It gave her a sort of strong yet ageless look that men were helpless against, and she was always followed around by one or two of the poor besotted fools.

Eight: The First Wrinkle

Not a fun occasion. Wrinkles are actually kind of neato, in a biology experiment sort of way, until you're 29 and counting. Then they're abominations. I mean, your acne scars only just now faded away. And now this?

Repeat this mantra: *French women spend the bulk of their makeup dollar on skin care products.* You must begin to do the same. This isn't hard to do if you, like me, gave up wearing large quantities of makeup in high school, and now find that a bottle of good-quality skin cream from Macy's costs upwards of

$40, which is about twice your makeup dollar for the year. Spend wisely.

Whatever you do, don't start thinking that you can turn back the ravages of time by silly actions like refusing to smile anymore. Those lines around your mouth, those crow's feet around your eyes, are just like roaches in a kitchen. If you've already seen them, they're there for good. Now is the time to read all the literature on how cultures other than ours admire wrinkles. Now is the time to stop buying those 1,000-watt bulbs for your bathroom mirror. Now is the time to start wearing sunblock religiously.

I must also point out that now it's payback time for all those girls in high school and college who could tan in minutes what it took you all summer to achieve. If you, like me, were laughed off the beach by our more olive-complected sisters, feel free to laugh back, and loudly. Those girls of summer, those Bain de Soleil–using, reflective-towel buying, string-bikini-wearing chicks who snorted at our alabaster legs and freckled faces, now are wishing they'd spent a little less time and a little less baby oil on the beach. When you see these chicks on the street now, make a point of greeting them warmly, with air kisses to both cheeks. Then make sure to loudly mistake them for their mothers. It's a horrible thing to do, but remember the Alamo, that's my motto.

Seven: The First Day Your Bones Ache

One day you will wake up and realize you have aches and pains that were not there before. Naturally, your first thought will be that you have bone cancer and just how bad can a year get anyway? It is probably not cancer or meningitis or anything like that. No, no. It's only the aging process knocking on your door to say hi. Now is the time when you can no longer pretend your body doesn't feel what you're doing to it. Now is the time your body comes back for revenge.

"What scares me is now when I go skiing and I fall, it really hurts," says Christy Harbreggar, 30. "Did it always hurt this much or did I just not notice it? I got into a really bad ski accident a few years ago, and now I have a bum knee. And that sounds like such an old person's thing, 'my bum knee.'"

Sorry ladies, but the aches and pains are here to stay. Now is a good time to look into those yoga classes you've been putting off since college, or to sign up for lap swimming. These things are good exercise and don't tend to make anything worse. Nothing need actually change for an average chick (excepting, as we've seen, ballet dancers and athletes—probably stuntchicks too), just keep in mind that you need to be a bit nicer to your poor, misunderstood, no-longer-22-year-old body.

For the record, it is wise to keep your suffering to yourself. You don't want to add verbal proof to anyone's perception of you as an aging being. When struggling to keep up in the company picnic relay race, or nursing your sprained ankle through its fourth week, simply smile and come up with another excuse for your lameness, such as lack of sleep the night before due to an overamorous male model you've been seeing. Never, under any circumstances, are you allowed to publicly utter "I'm just not as young as I used to be." You don't get to say such things until you actually start to look older, which for all of us except the most stressed out is probably not for another 15 or 20 years.

Remember what Confucius once said: "A wise man feels much but says little." Or something to that effect.

Six: Loss of Metabolism

I say the following not to gloat or inspire hatred but only to drive home a prescient point. So please read on to the end of the section before you pass harsh judgment on me and hurl this book to the floor.

I was always a thin woman. This thinness at first manifested itself in a body that refused to mature until well into high school and was the bane of my existence. I had legs so skinny that the boys would laugh at me whenever I had to show them, which was more often than I would have liked since I was on the drill team and had to wear stupid-looking short skirts half the week. My girlfriends at the time used to fast or purge for a day consuming nothing but fruit juice because it was thought to be healthy and a good test of will. I would follow their example until I'd pass out from low blood sugar and end up in bed, while my dad, all six foot four and no fat on him, lectured me on why I couldn't go a day without food like most girls. "You don't have the body fat," he'd say, handing me a glass of orange juice and a fried egg sandwich. I was a skinny girl.

In college it got better. I was skinny, but I grew some boobs and had a nice set of hips, even a butt that could pass muster. Throughout most of my 20s I enjoyed a body that remained naturally thin no matter how much I ate or how little I exercised. This put me in the minority of young women who were satisfied with their body weight, and indeed, I never gave it a thought. I figured every gal had to have at least one physical feature she was really pleased with, and since I wasn't blessed with thick curls or clear skin or cheekbones that could slice baloney, then it was only my due to be able to fit, at 27, into a miniskirt I bought when I was 19 at the Esprit outlet.

Hate my guts? Don't. None of the above applies any longer. My natural metabolism fled the scene right at 31 and has not been seen since. This is something everyone swore would happen, and I believed them not. I kept the Esprit outlet skirt, dubbed the diet skirt, around all these years, just to prove them wrong.

But by 32 I began to notice the chocolate bars I ate with such abandon were hanging around the hips. At a family reunion I suddenly had a grotesque moment of clarity and saw exactly where my body was headed—and it wasn't anywhere the diet skirt would be able to follow. These days, I sit on an extra 20 pounds. I have neither the discipline nor the stamina to get rid of them. In fact, after years of blissful ignorance about the wacky world of dieting and exercise, I'd say things don't look good for my former skinny self. Especially now that I'm over 30 and every time I try to stretch out my legs, I pull a tendon.

Now, sisters, is when the joke finally comes to roost on me and my skinny ilk. All those years we were blithely enjoying our French onion soup and rice pudding snacks were years we could have spent saving for the day when our metabolisms would leave us high and dry. We should have learned discipline. We should have learned restraint. We should have at least learned our calorie counts, but we didn't. And now, at 30, we're paying the price.

I have tried to see the good in this particular first. I have tried to reconcile myself to my exciting new "adult" woman's body, but somehow I just can't. Especially with all those slinky little black numbahs sitting in my closet that I can no longer get my butt into. Don't even mention the diet skirt. I may have to burn it.

Your metabolism will be leaving you soon as well. If it doesn't, and you're still able to eat all you want and stay as thin as you were at 22, then you're a good candidate for osteoporosis (just to give *you* something to worry about too).

But if you have been watching your weight all your life and eating with restraint, maybe even exercising regularly, God love you, then now is your time to revel. You're finally at ease with the body you got at birth and now all the skinny twits you hated all those years have caught up in weight and will soon surpass anything you'd ever let yourself become. Feh.

So you've lived through these various firsts. Now comes the headier stuff. The major life changes every chick naturally assumes will happen to her before the magic 30th birthday.

Five: Marriage

Chicks our age know a lot about marriage long before we're of an age to experience one ourselves. God knows most of our parents—both sets of them—have a lot of experience with it, including how to get out of it. So it's a little surprising that so many of us still have this romantic idea that marriage is something we'll do one day—preferably soon—and stay in until the day we die.

In popular marriage lore—the tacitly understood facts bandied about in single circles—marriages come in three waves. There is the after-college wave, all those sweethearts tying the knot weeks after graduation, to the joy of their parents and the skeptical smiles of everyone else. Most of these kids are ready for marriage number two right around 30, so feel free to snap up any old college flames at that time. Then there is the second wave of marriages, which usually hits critical mass between 25 and 28. These are a bit more easily swallowed by still-single friends. There is a chance that these matches, tempered by a few years' experience, might last longer. For those of you still single, these are much more disquieting than the first wave, which you dismissed with a snort and a laugh. Now, however, you're starting to worry. After this second wave, there is an unsettling between 28 and 32, when nobody seems to get hitched and which only adds to your suspicion that you have, in fact, missed the boat entirely. Happily, things appear to pick up from 32 onward, when people start to realize that it's time to grow up and take some responsibility for oneself. Peer pressure starts to work on guys at this point, prompting even the most roving commitmentphobe to find a suitable woman and settle down. Living together past this age begins to take on a tawdry, common-law sheen.

Regardless of the three-waves theory, many an otherwise levelheaded chick is horrified at reaching the age of 30 sans mate. This is because we've been socialized to think that 30 is the drop-dead cutoff for institutions like this (maybe they're worried we'll get hip to the scam if we get any older and wiser).

"Every cultural message we receive from the day we're born tells us that marriage is the place where we women will flourish; where we'll finally become "real women" and have social approval, sanctified sex, utter and total happiness," says Dalma Heyn, author most recently of *Marriage Shock*, who has researched and written about marriage for more than 10 years.

"To clinch the idea that we're nothing if we're unwed, this myth tells us that single women—dreaded, dried-up *spinsters*—are doomed to misery and loneliness, and are out there tearing their hair out until they can snag a husband."

Yikes. But let's be honest here. Fear of turning into one of those ladies with 10 cats is the fear. Even today this idea is so ingrained in us that we look at older single women, no matter how full and rich their lives are, and suppose that beneath it all they're unhappy and lonely without a mate. Maybe they are. But maybe they aren't. It's not something anyone can say for sure, right?

It doesn't help when the media comes out with superhyped faux surveys, like the one a few years back claiming that a woman who hits 40 and is still single is more likely to get hit by lightning than to find a husband. Who buys such rubbish? Apparently, a great many do, since this supposed scientific survey got more ink than World War II. It promptly took its place in the marriage myth. Who knows how many chicks went on Prozac because of that report?

Hah. Funny I should ask. Dig this: according to national statistics, married women are three times more depressed than their single sisters, and five times more depressed than married men.

"Men thrive in marriage," says Heyn. "Emotionally, physically, psychologically. They wither outside it. Married women and single men are the two most depressed segments of the population."

So you might ask yourself: what's the rush?

Despite all the white, fluffy feelings we get when we ponder nuptial bliss, marriage is still an inherently male institution. In *Marriage Shock*, Heyn goes into great detail about the expectations society has for those women who go on to become wives, and how lots of times these very expectations crush the spirits out of formerly happy, independent, fun-loving chicks. "The myth we so believe in has lied to us in order to lure women into an institution that was designed for the nurturance of men and children," she says. "This isn't to say women can't be happily married, but that—like the Army or the Church— marriage is a male institution. If we don't understand that, we'll never understand how to transform the institution into a place that's as nurturing to wives as it has long been for husbands and children."

Maybe being 30 and still single was a big deal in our mothers' generation, when all that was expected of women was to produce boy children and concoct a better Christmas cookie. But today, when a girl has to educate herself and then go out and arm herself with experiences both on the job and in life, 30 is a relatively young age to assume she's met the one she wants to spend the rest of it with by.

Statistics bear out the wisdom of waiting. Studies show that marriages made in your 30s are five times more likely to last 20 years than marriages made earlier. No doubt you have already seen this statistic in action.

Indeed, assuming you're finally starting to get your own life in order, why would you want to sign on with somebody who may expect you to move for their career, take their name, and join your hard-earned mutual fund with theirs? Unlike our mothers' generation, we're our own chick, thank you. Agree to become someone's partner, someone's soul mate. Never agree to become an appendage.

When you look at things this way, you will want to take your time and choose a mate, and choose wisely. By 30, you're only now getting hip to what you really want in a partner any-way. Think back on all the fun you had in your 20s, all that sowing of oats. All that dancing on bartops and showing your tits at Mardi Gras. Could you have done any of it with that acne-scarred, Camaro-driving little schmuck you were in love with in high school? Don't think so.

So in reality, the unmarried 30-year-old chick should be smarter than to be worried. Yes, it gets lonely out there some-times. Yes, being single can be fun on occasion but mostly mad-dening. And yes, it would just be fabu to meet Mr. Right and never have to worry about any of it anymore. But still we worry.

"It's amazing that we're doing things our mothers could never do, but we're still terrified of not being married by 30," says Andrea McGinty, 36, who owns a dating service and knows of what she speaks.

Besides. Once you set a date, you will be set upon by the wedding beast, the horrible specter of wedded bliss, that will insist that if you do not spend a year's salary or more on this one day you will never experience marriage as it was meant to be.

Our culture has a sick love/hate relationship with marriage. Fifty percent of all American marriages end in divorce, and yet the wedding business remains a billion-dollar industry. Those wedding magazines weighing down the newsstand—they're veritable tomes of how to spend your inheritance on the white wedding of your dreams.

How many of your girlfriends have fallen face first into the white wedding trap? Otherwise sensible chicks suddenly feel it's absolutely necessary to blow three months' salary on a dress they're going to wear exactly once and then consign to moth-balls. I don't buy the idea that every little girl daydreams about being a bride (I daydreamed about wearing anything with a hoop skirt), but that's the only explanation I have for this sudden dementia. Why else would anyone in their right mind think it's OK to spend $2,000 on flower bouquets?

I know far too many chicks who swore they would have sensible, small-scale wedding ceremonies only to find themselves screaming hysterically at the caterers who put a green garland on every plate instead of the blue one that matched the bridesmaids' dresses.

Don't even get me started on bridesmaids' dresses.

Personally, I've always admired people who went to the Elvis Chapel of Love or its equivalent in Vegas, or simply told it to the judge at city hall. Blow your wad on a party and a honeymoon, that's what I say. Leave the ceremony for the divorce.

Four: Babies

There are chicks out there who have babies by the time they're 30. This does not by any means suggest that they're not just as panicked at turning 30 as their child-free sisters are, it just means they're panicking for two. "Turning 30 took a total backseat to being pregnant," recalls Dawn Wallace, 31. "But now everything else, how tired I am, what shape my bod's in, is complicated by the fact that I had a baby. And every year I keep getting older on top of it."

I remember meeting a woman who expressed the very sentiment I'd always held, of having children before I was 30 or else. It was outside an art gallery in SoHo, where I'd just attended an art opening with friends who frequented this sort of thing and who were decidedly more downtown and hip than I was, and so I was feeling particularly vulnerable. A good-looking woman and her older, artist-type husband greeted my friends, whose circles they apparently ran in, and apologized because they had to leave early to relieve the baby-sitter. That started a whole conversation about progeny, of which the woman confessed that she'd gotten in just after the before-30 deadline. "I know it's silly," she shrugged, all blond hair and friendly self-deprecation. "But I really felt I had to have a baby before I turned 30. I had my son just two months after my birthday."

This story left my one girlfriend, a gorgeous 25-year-old, nonplussed. But it threw me into the depths of despair, knowing that I had virtually no chance of pulling off a similar feat, even if I got knocked up that night

It was a lot of worry for nothing. Listen up, while it's true that you're working under a deadline with this particular accomplishment, it's absolutely do-able if you apply the fundamentals of list making. If having a baby is the most important thing on your list at the moment, then set out to make it happen. Just because that biological clock is now ticking loudly it doesn't mean you'll die childless. It just means that you have to plan accordingly.

Sure, it might take you the remaining 10 years between now and the time you're 40 to meet a guy worth procreating with, but it could also happen overnight. I happen to know many women who went from swinging single gals to oatmeal swinging mothers in the space of one calendar year. In fact, such metamorphases happen all the time so there's no reason it won't happen to you. The really determined chick can do it in less time. All it requires is a total suspension of disbelief.

Besides, you really do have 15 years left, thanks to modern

science. Career women all over the country wait until they're in their 40s (or later) to reproduce, spending thousands of dollars trying to get themselves into a state they could have gotten in for the price of a drive-in movie back in their early 20s. Whole medical clinics are well-funded thanks to these women. And remember, if Murphy Brown can do it, so can you.

You must also let fate play a hand when you decide it's more or less time to have a baby. If you're married (or not, but have a responsible partner—that much you need) and one day the birth control goes out of whack and you find yourself preggers but not quite ready, take it as a sign and go for it. Convince the guy later. He's not going to do any of the dirty work anyway.

Debby Lovell, 32, just found out she was pregnant, not that they were planning it or anything. "I feel really ready for this experience and really ready for a child," she says. "Not necessarily prepared, but ready. I'm fairly sure my husband will come around."

Three: Home Ownership

There are people out there—most of them men—who feel that in order to be a fully functioning member of adult, over-30 society, a life-sucking mortgage is in order. As someone who has lived my entire adult life in cities where the average cost of a home equals three lifetimes of work for those of us in noninvestment-banking situations, I disagree. Home ownership is a state of mind.

There are several ways of looking at why you wouldn't want to own a house or other property before you're 30. Let's look at the first reality.

(A note: I address here those chicks who live in big metropolitan areas or booming regions, since I have no experience with what it's like to live in areas where housing is affordable and home ownership is routine among the under-30 set. I am talking to chicks who spend up to 50 percent of their after-tax paycheck on rent and have never known any other way. All of you enjoying life in the Midwest, kindly disregard this section.)

If you happen to have inherited a home or work in a field that enables you to buy a home prematurely, you will be hated by all your peers and automatically cast from all boomer-bashing sessions. You can not be one of us if you are one of *them*, and home ownership turns you into one of *them* faster than any known condition on earth. Inheritance of home ownership is only a slightly lesser offense in the eyes of tenants, since it means your parents were the same boomer scum who profited on cheap real estate in the '60s and raised rents in the '80s and '90s for the rest of us.

Home ownership at an unseemly age also makes you highly suspect in the eyes of everyone else—even other adults. It's just never wise to draw attention to your drug cartel connections, your trust fund, or your Ponzi scheme.

Barring inheritance or obscene pay, you may still opt to purchase a home, but it will almost certainly be out in the deepest, darkest suburbs and will most certainly be a more shoddily built replica of the tract home you grew up in. Maybe it will have a cathedral ceiling. It will be in a development with some horrible name like Babbling Willows or Remote Spotte, and you will, in exchange for affordability, be required to drive two hours to reach civilization of any kind, including your job.

Also in exchange, you will by necessity have to put aside all childish things we under-30s still desperately cling to. You will not be able to leave town on a moment's notice. You can't decide to join the Peace Corps one night without months of hassle figuring out what to do with your house. Your weekends will be spent landscaping or repairing roofs. You will suddenly start caring about scintillating adult issues such as property taxes and theft insurance. In short, you will have willingly become the suburban nightmare of your youth.

My advice to you: don't do it. Delay gratification until you can live where you want to live (you may have to wait a long time). Or convince yourself, as I have, that home ownership as part of the American Dream didn't apply until after World War II, when cheap housing, and lots of it, suddenly became available to the masses returning home and availing themselves of government loans. Before then, only the truly well-off could afford a home of their own. Generations grew up happy and healthy in rentals. We can too.

Two: *Nicht eine Wunderkind*

Let's just admit it. For a lot of us ambitious, career-minded types, occupational glory could only be fully achieved and properly savored if we could say we were under 30 when we did it. It doesn't help that the media loves a *wunderkind* and never hesitates to let us know that so-and-so was 26 when he produced his first play or that at 28 she was the youngest brain surgeon at Mt. Sinai. The first novel has practically become a genre unto itself, with every new writer hailed as the next Fitzgerald. In my case, just finding out that an author of a best-selling book was born in 1970 throws me into a funk for the rest of the week. And it's not just writers. Every glam field is filled with under-30 *wunderkinds* that we all assumed we'd join the ranks of once out of college.

But now it's too late. We've missed our chance to be mentioned in our local papers as the local girl made good.

A chick who spends more than a few minutes bumming over this needs to have her Cape Cod thrown on her. Really.

One of the true blessings of getting older means you start to experience a more relaxed way of looking at things like this. At first this can be alarming, especially for those of us who spent our 20s flying from one insane drama to the next. But even though you thought such an attitude was the mark of mediocrity and proof of impending old age back when you were 20, you'll grow to like it as soon as you pass 30. It's like a narcotic. It's nice. It grows on you. It makes life a lot easier.

It doesn't mean that you don't care anymore. It just means you're more realistic. We all need to remind ourselves that these brilliant young minds we always read about are about .001 percent of the population. We're reading about them precisely because they've done jaw-droppingly well for themselves at such an early age. The rest of us laboring in obscurity don't make good copy.

Besides, apart from the one or two truly genius types (who have lousy social lives anyway), think about what it takes to hit the big time in most fields apart from maybe music and Hollywood, which I'll explain later. It takes blind devotion, naked ambition, and obsession that obliterates all else. Not attributes that generally make up a good dinner date. I happen to know several guys and at least one chick in their 20s who are engaged in starting up their own businesses. All four of them readily admit that they have absolutely no life outside of work, and realize that it must be thus if they are to make a go of it. So when you read about how one of them just made $10 trillion in the IPO of the century, realize that they sacrificed all the stuff that makes youth so much fun. No spending all day in bed with a new lover. No six-month trekking trips in exotic locales. No impromptu weekend road trips. True, this person now has more money than God, but rest assured that she has lost all sense of how to relax and really enjoy it in the process.

Now making it in the music business, especially in popular music, seems to be mostly based on luck and looks. Ever notice how every hot new female vocalist discovered also happens to have bee-stung lips and good bones? Is it a coincidence that Jewell, Alanis Morissette, and Fiona Apple all look like models? Call me cynical (go on, I'll take it as a compliment), but if MTV ever let a plain girl make a video I'd eat my clicker. But I digress. Perhaps more important than even looks in the music industry today is youth. This is a nonnegotiable prerequisite. Unless of course you happen to be the Rolling Stones, and those other geezers from the '60s who continue to tour even though they penned immortal phrases like "Hope I die before I get old. . . ."

Hollywood too. You gotta be young. And you gotta be pretty. It helps to have some talent, but it's not absolutely necessary. It also helps to be related to someone already in Hollywood. Just wait; in not too many more years we will be treated to one of Bruce Willis and Demi Moore's daughters telling a fan magazine that her being cast in the latest blockbuster had nothing to do with who her parents are and everything to do with hard work and dedication to the high art of the cinema. You wait.

But otherwise, it's a big race to the finish line in most nonglam professions I can think of. And why? Did this idea that anybody worth anything must make their first million before they were 30 exist before the '80s?

Whatever happened to the idea of slow but steady winning the race? Tragically unhip, I know, but still sound. There is a dignity to winning your 15 minutes of fame after a lifetime of hard work and effort, and particularly of not winning that fame at all. I still hold strong to the romantic and noble notion of unsung labor, and let's face it: it's the lot of most people in the world. No shame in being part of that. Life offers its own rewards.

But let's say for argument's sake that your 15 minutes of fame do come, and come way early in the game, like in your mid-20s. What happens then? You spend the rest of what should be your developing career trying to maintain that level of achievement, and this, the cosmos tells us, is doomed to fail. What nobody tells earnest overachievers (who wouldn't listen anyway, no doubt) is that early success has a built-in counterpoint. And even more than it loves a *wunderkind*, the media loves a fallen *wunderkind*. It makes for even better, bitchier copy when the young star can't quite live up to his or her first effort. Look what happened to the literary brat packers Brett Easton Ellis and Tama Janowitz. Whither goest? Twenty-something film director Harmony Korine, the guy who did the gross but critically acclaimed *Kids*, just released *Gummo*, to universal revile. The media creates the monster, but then it eats its young. Let's just hope Tiger Woods keeps his handicap.

Think of it as saving yourself a lot of public and personal scrutiny. I can't imagine a worse pressure than having to outdo

myself after winning a Pulitzer Prize at 27. (Well, yeah, of
course it would have been nice.)

One: An Established Career

So you're 30 and you work in a video store. So what? Maybe
this new reality will prompt you to work toward becoming the
owner of the video store. Maybe your screenplay will sell.
Maybe you're just a person who's content to work in a video
store.

There's way too much din in our society aimed at telling us
what we should have accomplished by a certain age. I think
we're free to ignore it. We're certainly free to start ignoring it
by the time we're 30.

Believe me, a lot of the people who got nice, responsible
jobs right out of college are envying you. They would never
dare admit it, as they drive their new cars or tell you about the
house they're planning to buy. But you know that despair that
creeps into your soul after your second day of corporate temping? That's what these chicks are feeling in the middle of the
night, when they lie staring at the ceiling in the darkness and
feel their lives slipping away in the monotony of their daily
grind. Even those who seem to be smitten with what they do
must ask themselves whether there isn't something more to life
than work. They must see the petty politics, the deceits, the
strange alliances inherent in corporate America. Unless they're
on Prozac or just too soulless to realize, they must ask themselves for what they are working, day in and day out, as their
youth speeds by. More stuff? A gold watch when (and if) they
retire? You, by comparison, aren't plagued by thoughts like these
in the wee hours of the night. Maybe over how you're going to

make rent this month, but never anything deeper than that. Count yourself lucky. Every day for you is a new adventure.

There is a whole school of thought that asks why one needs to live to work when one can work to live. This is very un-American, and if this were the '50s I'm sure I'd get called in by the feds or get blacklisted as a commie sympathizer. It's the kind of attitude you see more in Europe, which goes along with all their good food and cheeses and wine and cigarettes and why they seem to enjoy life a lot more than we do. But it's always had its followers here in the States, and I think their numbers are growing. Particularly in our generation, which hasn't been given any reason at all to devote our lives to the corporation, and those of us who aren't motivated by money.

"I'm not a career person, I'm sure of that," says Keri Burrett, who is 30 and just starting her studies to get a teaching certificate. "I'm sure teaching will be between five and ten years and then I'll do something else. In my 20s I wanted to do volunteer stuff in other countries and I just checked out all kinds of things to do, but you know, the student loans came up and having to pay the bills, and I couldn't work for free, so it was like, OK, so I found other ways of doing kind of interesting things."

The chick who works to live, then, wants a life. She doesn't want to get tied down into a 9 to 5 that doesn't mean anything to her, and she can not be enticed into it by the promise of money. This is a chick who has a rich and meaningful relationship with everything else she does outside the eight hours or so a day she has to work to pay the rent. Maybe she publishes a 'zine. Or paints murals. Or choreographs for youth groups. She doesn't define herself by what she does in her job but rather by what she does in life. And whatever she does, this chick has made the choice to live as she does, and she lives well, and she is happy. Yes, happy. Even without a new car every year or a Club Med vacation. Happy even though she hasn't invested a cent in the stock market. There seems to have been a brief time in the '60s when it was OK to live like this, but that time lives on only in the collective memory of aging boomers stuck in traffic while on hold with their brokers on the car phone. The chick who chooses to live this lifestyle today must forever put up with disapproving clucks from the rest of the consumer culture.

An added bonus I've found: if you do anything long enough, remunerative rewards will eventually come your way, whether you want them to or not. Look what happened to Quentin Tarantino—a video store employee for many moons.

OK, you want a more realistic example. I know a chick, a painter in her early 30s, who scratched out the most meager of livings for herself throughout her 20s by working in frame shops. She complained only when the rest of us did, and the rest of the time made due with her $5-an-hour job plus whatever other odd thing she could get: posing for art classes, cleaning up after gallery openings, that sort of thing. She put up with all sorts of hassle from her folks, who wanted to know why she didn't get a real job with the college education they had bought her. One day someone happened to see her portfolio lying on the counter in the frame shop and, impressed with her work, offered my girlfriend a teaching gig. Suddenly, this chick who knew how to live close to the ground and make due with less had more money than she knew what to do with. Of course, no businessman would be able to pay his maid on what her salary was, but to her it was a windfall. She was on her way. And she hadn't even been looking.

You think I'm done? There's another component to all of this. One that conveniently comes into play for all of the above-mentioned sections: by the time you're 30, you really don't care much what people think anymore.

Your teens and 20s are spent loudly trying to convince everyone around you that you don't care what they think about you, when in fact the opposite is true. You care so much, particularly when you're a teenager, that whole books have been written about self-esteem problems caused by the rejection teenagers often face from their peer group. In your 20s you may still cling to the myth that you're a lone wolf, an independent mind out to do your own thing, but appearances still desperately count for a lot. What's the first thing one asks upon meeting another person of similar background? "What do you do?" or "Where did you go to school?" Answers to questions like these reveal volumes, and you can then start to rank this new person accordingly, and see where you stack up.

The whole turning-30 trauma is the last, dramatic flare-up of such urges, I promise. You go through a year of hell comparing yourself to every other 29-year-old on the planet, and then you just stop caring. This is one of the best-kept secrets of aging. It's the natural narcotic of the over-30 set. It's why most people grow out of partying by the time they're 30 or so. And you were worried.

5 COPING

Tips for Girls Who Can't Afford the Prozac

What keeps a woman young and beautiful is not repeated surgery but perpetual praise.

Quentin Crisp

Chicks are pretty good at coping. And with all the drama inherent in life as a female, it's no wonder we've had to develop such skills. Whether it be surviving a broken heart or learning how to live with a subpar haircut, there is a long and historic body of knowledge we chicks have passed down from generation to generation. Often this knowledge includes the therapeutic use of chocolate items and three-hour hot baths with lots of expensive French bath balms and body scrubs and ten-inch all-natural loofahs. Sometimes it includes measures bordering on voodoo, such as writing the name of the banished on the skin of an onion and then boiling it until it disappears. Coping can be an ugly business. But we do what we need to, no?

My favorite coping story concerns an anonymous chick. A girlfriend of mine reported seeing a beautiful young woman walk into the restaurant she was dining at. The woman had great piles of blond hair that was so striking that half the patrons of the place, a fancy hotel restaurant in Los Angeles, were gawking at her from behind their menus, trying to place her in the pantheon of starlets. The woman asked the waiter to bring her one of every cocktail listed on the cocktail specials menu. When they arrived, all seven of them, in bright and unnatural hues with umbrellas in odd-shaped glasses, she very methodically began to go through each drink set before her. After about the third, she looked up and noticed my friend staring. She smiled sadly. "Just got dumped," she said, shrugging her shoulders. She returned to her drinks. "Wow," remarked my friend. "What a gal."

The Web We Weave

It's not so surprising then, that in this new and exciting communications age, some chicks have gotten very creative when coping with the trauma of turning 30. A case in point is Drue Miller, the webmistress at Vivid Communications in San Francisco. Writing and designing for the World Wide Web is one of the few areas of high-tech that is notably chick-friendly. It's also a very young industry, and in turn, its young turks tend to be twenty-somethings. Turning 30, which had always seemed so unlikely, gave her pause to think.

"In the months prior to my 30th birthday, it was starting to sink in. I remember waking up the month before and thinking, wow, 29 days left. I was starting to think about these sorts of things because 30 had always seemed so old. Now I was realizing that, you know, it's just one day, where I click over from my 20s to my 30s."

As a geekgirl, Drue had a lot of ways to deal with her problems. She could spend the day tearing around San Francisco on her motorcycle. She could lose herself for days in a particularly colorful and violent computer game. Or she could write her feelings out and design a website around them. She chose the latter, writing her fears away.

"Actually, that wasn't the only reason," she admits. "The real reason was my boyfriend was starting a 'zine, and we needed material for it, and I said well, I'm turning 30, that's an interesting story."

So she wrote a story about her thoughts on turning 30, everything from the small wrinkles appearing at the corners of her eyes to her ravenous new sex drive. She then created a post, a link to her story asking transient web surfers about their own take on aging. "Which birthday was most significant for you? Do you feel younger or older than you really are? How old is old, anyway? And how do you know when you've crossed that line?"

The result? More than 60 pages of responses from people all over the world—men and women—about turning 30, even though that wasn't specifically the question. And every day it grows. That's the beauty of interactive media, people can continue to empathize with a piece long after it's written. "I turned 30 almost two years ago," says Drue. "And I still get e-mail about that story." The posting continues to grow as well, with stories from all sorts of folks about to turn 30 who've been trolling the Net in search of succor.

And talk about succor. Reading some of the posts can make a gal feel almost happy about turning 30. At least you're in good company. Check out the post at http://www.fray.com/

drugs/30/post and read what you will. Here are a couple of samples:

When I hit 30 I thought of it as the horror of all horrors because I felt that anyone over 30 was over the hill. Well, when I hit 40 last year, I realized that maybe the best is yet to come. My 30s were really good years, and I accomplished a lot of things that I never thought I would. I was worried that after 30 I would start looking like my mother. Well, far from it. I get comments all the time from people who don't believe me when I tell them my age. I am probably in better shape physically, intellectually, emotionally, and spiritually than I was when I was in my 20s. Drue, it only gets better. I have much more self-confidence and assurance than at any time in my life. One thing to remember, Drue, is that the over-30 fallacy began back in the times when people only lived to be about 40–50 years old. The life span has been expanded by about 30 years now, so middle age is now much later than it used to be. People need to let go of those old stereotypes and enjoy life to the fullest each and every beautiful year and not worry about age. I'm 41 and proud of it.

—*Charlene*

What is going to happen when I turn 30? I am 26 and feel so old. It hit me two summers ago when I had a "girls weekend out" with my best friends from high school. They were all single, wild, and free. No worries, just out to have fun, able to party till the sun came up. I was married at 21, had my first baby at 23, and at 24 I was *old*. I envy the life of my single friends whose age doesn't seem to bother them. This year I had my second child. My girlfriends are still talking about dating and clubs, etc. I am talking about dinner, diapers, kids, the dog. I sure hope when I turn 30 it will get better. I know it will. When I am 30 I will have my little family and feel satisfied that I have done it all. My girlfriends may first be starting. When I am 30, I will feel my life will begin again. My children will be old enough to fend for themselves and I will be able to enjoy life . . . all of it!

—*Laura*

Listening to St.-John's-Wort

These are the times that try a chick's soul. Sometimes coffee, cigarettes, or whatever vice you'll own up to just aren't enough to keep your demons at bay, especially the kind that come at life-questioning, soul-searching times like around your 30th birthday. Sometimes a gal needs a little extra help coping.

Far be it from me to judge a chick who feels she needs to medicate her feelings into submission. Although I personally find the idea of millions of people living the rest of their lives on Prozac alarming, it's not for me to tell anyone how to live or what to ingest. God knows I spent many a night crying in loneliness and many mornings trying to find one good reason to get out of bed and face the day. But I always managed to pull out of these funks in a day or two, and always chalked them up to the almost-30/single/career chick in New York malaise. I did, however, know one or two women who could not pull out of these depressions, and who spent too much time in mental misery when by all outward appearances they should have been doing cartwheels. I know there are reasons for medication. I just think too many people have jumped on the Prozac bandwagon, such as it is.

But there are intriguing new and natural ways to beat the occasional blues. Chief among them is St.-John's-wort, a weed (literally) that's been used for centuries in Germany for its properties as a natural antidepressant. The Germans, in fact, prescribe it far more frequently and long before prescribing anything more synthetic to those with depression. Here in this country, it's been around for years, but hasn't been too well known outside of granola circles until recently. Venture into any health food store worth its tofu and look for it either as a tea or in capsules.

What makes it work? Since researchers in this country have only just started to give credence to natural remedies, they admit they don't rightly know. But it's been known to fight back the winter blahs, the menstrual blues, and the general mental blasé.

"I drink it in tea every winter and I swear to God it helps me through it," says Sandra Richter, 32, a teacher in Philadelphia who says she got turned on to St.-John's-wort during college in California. "It doesn't have a huge effect, but I've noticed it evens out my moods."

Although the popular wisdom says you have to take St.-John's-wort several times a day for several weeks to really feel the full effect, it seems to improve my moods right from the first pill. Perhaps I'm just peculiarly prone to suggestion, but a chick should try it and judge for herself.

As far as anyone knows, the downsides to St.-John's-wort are few, compared to the sinister effects of Prozac and its ilk (libido death, for example). It appears to make a user more sensitive to the sun, but then any chick nearing 30 should be long over her bake-in-baby-oil days anyway. Chicks who are pregnant or nursing should obviously refrain as well. As with any sort of medical advice, it's smart not to listen to people like me, who don't have medical degrees or indeed the fortitude to withstand even a basic blood test. So don't take what I say here as gospel. And unless you speak and read German and can look up relevant safety studies there, use it with caution, OK?

Good Vibrations

In grad school I lived in a student housing suite with 12 women of varying disciplines. There was a biology student, a poet, a film student, a law student (although we almost never saw her), a social work student, a couple of future policy wonks, and others. We lived in various combinations in rooms off a single living area that was, due to high cable costs, sans TV. This made for a lot of loafing and hanging around talking and comparing workloads. We were all different ages and from a wide swatch of backgrounds, and nothing brought us together like the Good Vibrations catalog.

Once upon a time there were a couple of chicks in San Francisco who thought what the world needed was a way for women to buy sex toys without having to venture into any dark, sticky porn shops filled with questionable, dark, and sticky men. They created the first ever "for women, by women" sex shop, a happy little sun-filled storefront in a safe, friendly neighborhood in San Francisco (and where else would you start a women-friendly sex store but?). Business was good, but it really took off when they started shipping a catalog to anyone who wanted it, and chicks were suddenly free to choose a vice in the comfort of their own homes and have it shipped to them in a plain brown wrapper.

It was the social worker who received the catalog. Once every month or so she'd discreetly knock on our respective doors. "Catalog's here," she'd say, and it was understood—we'd bring our checkbooks and meet in the pink-walled living room to huddle over the table.

Oh, the treasures within! They brought a tear of happiness to a single girl's eye. There, in tasteful ink illustrations, were vibrators of all shapes and sizes and colors. There was the Pinky, which was affordable at less than $10 and could discreetly pass for a tampon holder in your purse. For the more demanding, there was The Great King, nine inches of clear latex that was worth worshipping if you weren't inclined to run screaming from the room instead. There were other contraptions as well, designed to serve every taste and fancy of the modern woman. And a complete library of erotica. And a list of porn films, with commentary ("Zero plot but hot hot hot!").

It didn't matter whether you planned to buy nothing or start your own franchise, the Good Vibrations catalog was oftentimes just a chance for us chicks to get together and be raunchy. A wise woman (I'm not sure which one) once said that the key to staying young and gorgeous is maintaining a youthful irreverence. Once you banish things like the Good Vibrations catalog from your life, you will almost certainly find yourself pricing lovely split-level ranch homes in distant suburbs, and you will begin to look like your mother (assuming your mother doesn't get her own copy of the catalog). This is sage advice, indeed. It's lovely little details like this that bring us girls together and make us very glad indeed to be over the age of consent.

Ask Isadora

Ask someone who knows. Ask someone with a lot of framed degrees on her wall. Beware, though, sometimes not even the most qualified people, psychologists and that sort, can help you when you come to them with turning-30 angst. Some, usually aging boomer types, will spit on you and tell you to go away and return with a real problem, like what to do when you can't find parts for your minivan anymore.

Others, however, are not only more gracious, but they have some answers. Isadora Altman, for example, has been everywhere and done all of that and gives good advice to those who question. She's a board-certified sexologist and lifestyle columnist for a number of alternative weekly newspapers across the country, including the *San Francisco Bay Guardian* and *Time Out New York*. Every week she soothes the savage souls of readers who write her with all manner of problems ranging from the sublime to the ridiculous and back again. We humbly approached her and begged her to dispense some advice our way, a request she mercifully agreed to.

Q: Isadora, why, oh why are we so freaked out by this idea of turning 30? Can you shed some enlightenment?

A: Gladly. Still roaming around in the subconscious of this generation, even if it wasn't their use, is: "Never trust anybody over 30." Thirty's been that line between being young enough to get away with whatever, to no longer being young enough to get away with whatever, to being "You should know better by now." People start asking why you don't know what you want to be yet when you grow up. That puts a lot of responsibility onto the shoulders of the 30-year-old that he or she just may not be ready for. Also, women have that enormously fretting biological clock. If she's nowhere near interested in getting married, she knows that she only has a few more years to find that man and start her family or else that's it.

Q: Can we mere mortals prevent 30 from happening?

A: No you can't. But a person who is distressed by this milestone can simply move it up. They can say, all right, adulthood for me begins at 35. Or, I'm not gonna worry about this for another five years.

For example, when I hit 33, I liked 33. It seemed to me a good, proper age, you know, old enough and not old enough. So I had my annual 33rd birthday for several years. Thirty does not automatically confer wrinkles, gray hair, droopy skin, and so on. It's simply a number.

Q: Is it healthy and normal to suffer through a pre-30 countdown?

A: Not if you're scaring yourself with it, no. If your countdown means that you'd better hurry up and earn your first million, or hurry up and get pregnant, or get that great raise, if you're scaring yourself into some sort of action, then no, I don't think that's healthy. It's normal, because we all abuse ourselves verbally all the time. But it's not very healthy.

Q: Agreed. But try and stop it. It's like a bad George Michael song—it just keeps playing and playing in your head and you're powerless to stop it. What's a chick to do?

A: It does help enormously to set some realistic goals. In the year in which I am 30, you can tell yourself, I will . . . not date anybody who doesn't want to start a family. I will . . . ask for a raise and if I don't get it in X amount of time, I'll start looking for another job. I'm going to . . . see if I can afford even a closet, but live by myself and not with a horde of roommates. Whatever it is, make it quantifiable. In other words, knowing if you're happy or not is hard, but you know if you got that raise or not. It's a goal you can set for yourself, as opposed to scaring yourself by saying, "I'd better do something in the next five months, four months, three months . . . or else!" Or else what? You'll be miserable. That's what.

A Bit of Good Advice

If you can't find a therapist for advice, then you'll just have to turn to your friends and suck them for whatever tidbits they have. Sometimes, however, if you're acting really morose, they'll find you.

In the days leading up to my 30th birthday, I roamed my place of employ in a daze. I was known for killing entire eight-hour blocks with nonstop socializing. It was kind of work, although more like networking. I'd go from office to office, ostensibly to ask an art director if, say, she thought a chart or a graph was more appropriate to the particular story being illustrated, and then spend the next 40 minutes yakking about whether Tommy Tune had any chance of a comeback. I spent more than one hour of every day downstairs getting coffee with various people, and the few times I sat for extended periods in my own office an almost steady stream of visitors made work nearly impossible. In retrospect, this probably had something to do with my failure to make anything of myself while at *Business Week*. But at least I was well liked while I floundered.

So it should not have surprised me when the ladies showed up en masse in my office that day. These women I worked with were journalists, editors, and art directors. The youngest was three years older than I; the oldest, 20 years my senior. Some were married, some divorced, some always single. They were all what I considered hip, urbane, together women, and worthy of anyone's admiration. They had noticed, they said, that I was not my usual chipper self, and they suspected it might have something to do with a certain arbitrary birthday fast approaching.

At first I denied it. It was the ultimate in lost face to admit that a little thing like turning 30 actually bothers you. But these chicks weren't fooled. Joni said it first, not surprisingly. "C'mawn," she said, "why deny it? Nobody wants to turn 30, because you don't know any better before then." She was in her mid-40s, a top financial editor, single. She used to regale me with tales of her globe-trotting and bed-hopping as we furtively smoked cigarettes in her office on deadline night. Joni was someone you had to listen to because you knew that no matter what your problem was, she'd been there, done that. Several times over. "Listen, kid," she said in a conspiratorial whisper, "your early 30s are the best years of your life as a woman. You've been around long enough so that people respect what you do, but you're still young and sexy and all that. So knock this misery crap off right now and start enjoying it." The others nodded in agreement.

Well. That's the first time I'd ever heard that. In fact, up until that very minute, I'd never given a thought to what life would actually be like *après* 30. I'd only concentrated on what everyone had always *told* me it would be like: resigned; lost potential; dull haircuts.

But apparently this wasn't the case, judging from the stories these women were laying on me. One by one they stepped forward and dispensed their wisdom. "Guaranteed, great things will happen for you between now and 33," swore one chick, one of the best reporters on the magazine. "Every single woman I know went through what you're going through, and every one of them had something great happen to them after they turned 30." She sounded very sure of herself. I wondered if she'd actually done research.

They told me about women who married and got pregnant within a year after turning 30. They told me about women who quit their horrible accounting jobs and went on to open successful restaurants. One told me that her girlfriend, an attorney, decided at 31 that what she really wanted to do—all her life— was throw pottery. Her parents and colleagues were livid when she told them of her plans, but she felt that she had proved everything she'd set out to prove as a professional, and had earned the right to live for herself. "She actually quit her job, sold everything she owned, and went and apprenticed with a master potter in Japan," my friend told me. "Nobody could believe it. But she's so happy she doesn't care." I didn't really believe it, either, but I got the point she was aiming at. One of the art directors said she didn't have any glamorous tales. But she and all her friends found that after 30, it became easier to accept themselves for who they were and not what they'd always planned on being. "You definitely grow into yourself," she said.

This talking-to actually helped. A lot. All these women couldn't be wrong, right? If it had happened to them, surely it could happen to me as well. And when it didn't, I could say I told you so with impunity. Except everything they spoke of came to pass. When wiser women than you speak, listen.

Group Bitch

A coffee klatch. A kvetch session. A group bitch. Talking your fears away is a time-honored chick's method for achieving peace of mind. Or piece of mind.

So with this in mind, four of us got together at Dawn's house one summer Sunday afternoon. There is Dawn, an artist and graphic designer who's just turned 31 and recently had her first child. There is me, 32 at the time. There are two of Dawn's girlfriends, met on a temp assignment long ago. Keri just turned 30 this summer and is handling it pretty well, except that it's prompted her to question what society is expecting from her versus what she expects from herself. Frances is staring 29 in the face and isn't happy about it one bit. Dawn rents a small house right on the beach in Oxnard, California with her construction worker/surfer husband. From their porch you can see the dirt lot where the surfers all park their trucks to surf Silver Strand, as this section of beach is known. Sometimes you can even see their girlfriends, all of them 20-year-old *Baywatch* types. We avert our eyes and order veggie burgers from the joint down the street. We've come to talk about being 30, growing older, and related topics. To start the conversation, though, we call over to Dawn's 15-year-old cousin, who's staying with her for a few weeks from Michigan. She's putting on makeup and curling her hair, preparing to venture outside to the beach, where she might meet a surfer. Her pastel-colored beeper is clipped neatly to her bikini bottom. She primps and watches MTV at the same time. "Hey Michelle," Dawn starts. "What do you think about turning 30?" We're looking for some perspective here.

Michele's eyes never leave the TV. "I don't think about turning 30," she says.

"Well," I say. "That pretty much sums it up. We can leave now."

Instead, we start to talk. Frances, it seems, is truly upset at the idea of turning 29, largely because it hints at the likelihood of turning 30 a year later, and she feels like she hasn't done anything with her life. What she doesn't mention until later is that she grew up on an Okinawa air force base, the daughter of a Japanese mother and an American serviceman. Or that her high school years were spent at the American High School in Alexandria, Egypt, alongside the kids of diplomats, foreign correspondents, and oil sheiks. Not exactly a dull upbringing. But that's the problem, she insists. The momentum was there, she just didn't take advantage of it. One of her temp gigs turned permanent, and now she's stuck in the accounting department in the headquarters of a large chain of copy shops—an awful fate, we agreed. But otherwise, she seems to have a lot going for her. She's happily married, she's articulate, she looks about 23 years old.

"So Frances," I start. "Why this panic?"

Frances rolls her eyes and throws her chin into her cupped hands. "The years are going by like weeks," she says. "I don't know what happened. The last birthday I remember is 21, and since then they've whizzed by." She'd made a list, all right, of things to do before she hit 30, but it remained largely undone. "And now I'm going to be 29 and I have one year left."

"What was on your list?"

"Let's see, I was going to go to college and graduate. I was going to write a book and publish it. I was going to do more traveling. I was *not* going to get married. That I did do. And I was *not* going to have a corporate job; that I did do, too."

I stare at her. "You're married and you have a good job," I say. "What a wretched existence. I should have been so lucky when I was 29."

"No, listen," says Frances. "Most people choose a career path when they're in their 20s, and they spend their 30s implementing it. Not that many people switch when they hit their 30s, so it's like I have a limited amount of time to make that switch. That's what that ticking sound is to me."

Dawn's been pulling cutlery out of the reach of her six-month-old son, Kyle, and listening to all of this. "You've got plenty of time, Frances."

Frances shakes her head. "I don't think so. Look at all the people who've lived and died before they're 30. Who've accomplished so much: Janis Joplin, Jim Morrison, all of those people died way before they were 30."

"So you want to OD?" We laugh. Dawn points to the kitchen. "There's some Jim Beam in the cupboard," she says helpfully.

"What I'm trying to say here is that holding down the kind of corporate job I have now is not what I expected to be doing back when I was 18 or 19," says Frances. "It's depressing. If I had had any idea I'd end up doing this I think I would have offed myself."

"Don't talk like that," says Keri. "You can change anytime you want."

"No I can't," says Frances. "I'm married. Happily married. And sometimes I think that Charlie is the only thing that stands between me and certain death." She laughs.

I point out that she made the choice of true love over care-free wanderlust and that a chick can generally only do one choice at a time. She considers this. Keri, meanwhile, tells us that as far as the choice thing goes, she's enjoying the smorgasbord.

"All through my 20s I just checked out all kinds of different things," she says. "That's one of the reasons I don't think turning 30 freaked me out as much as some people, because I feel like I did a lot of things I wanted to do." Sure, now there's pressure to be responsible and settle down, have kids, start a savings account, she says. But she's ignoring the call for now. She's living with her boyfriend, Tom, for the time being, even though this is frowned upon in her strictly Christian family. Nor does the biological clock tick particularly loud for her. "I have to say that in my late 20s I was hearing it loud and clear," she tells us. "But now I feel it's kind of a choice, not so much a mandate. And especially now with the fertility drugs. You can have children up until your 50s, even 60s."

"I dunno about that," says Dawn, pulling her earring out of her son's mouth. "I'm only 31 and it's taking a lot out of me."

"It's just another choice you can make. You didn't have any of these choices 30 years ago. Now, the sky's the limit. It's almost like a mantle of responsibility. For a while after I graduated from college, I felt this huge expectation that I was supposed to do something important with myself. And now I kind of realize I'm gonna do what I want to do, and not what somebody else wants me to do. I really don't care what anyone thinks about me anymore, that's one of the things I liked about turning 30." She pokes at Frances. "And you should keep that in mind, girlie."

At this point Dawn's parents return from a sight-seeing trip in their Winnebago. They are in their 70s. Her stepmom carries a yappy little dog under her arm. Her dad has on Bermuda shorts. They are from Michigan, remember. "Why all the long faces, girls?" he booms.

"We're talking about turning 30, Dad," says Dawn.

"You're 30 already?" He looks confused for a moment, then waves his hand, dismissing the matter. "You're still kids. Now what's for lunch?" The group bitch is over. For now.

Write It Down

"Very cathartic," said my friend Emily Schwartz, 31, when I asked her to write down her turning-30 experiences. "I would highly recommend it."

Now, granted, Emily is a journalist. One who took her laptop with her on her year-long travel stint and somehow found outlets in which to log on in such unlikely places as Tonga and Fiji, so she could regale the rest of us with her marvelous travelogues. But I guess she never thought turning 30 was much of a story. Not until she began writing it down and unwittingly tapped into an emotional motherlode.

Just as making a list helps you sort out the clutter that is your life, a good daily rant in your journal is worth at least two

10 Things You Don't Have to Do Just Because You're 30

Cynthia Heimel said it best with this old adage: God protects drunks, infants, and girls who fear nothing and are up for anything. Write this adage down and keep it handy at all times. It will help you keep calm as you rapidly approach 30 and begin to panic.

1. Don't panic.

2. Don't decide that your life has been wasted because you're 30 and haven't produced an indie film yet.

3. Don't tell yourself it's time to get serious. It's rarely time to get serious.

4. Don't think it's "too late" to do anything, because the only time it's too late is when you're dead. Even then, you never know.

5. Don't start wearing sensible shoes.

6. Don't think you can't get away with hip-huggers and wrap-dresses just because you're 30. Remember, you were a little kid during the real '70s; hence you have insight. Not to mention that authentic mood ring.

7. Do not, under any circumstances, start acting your age.

8. Don't take out your nipple ring just yet.

9. Don't stop having crushes on inappropriate boys.

10. Don't forget to invite your girlfriends to your Third Annual 29th Birthday Party next year.

medium-priced therapists in value. You can tell a journal everything you can tell a therapist, and more. There are no personality conflicts with your journal. Your journal won't interrupt you in the middle of a weepy harangue about your father to tell you that your hour is up. There is absolutely no risk of falling in love with your journal, or of your journal falling in love with you. Best of all, you would be hard-pressed to spend more than $45 on a journal (and we're talking a leather-bound volume with perfumed, handmade paper), whereas any therapist worth her couch bills at least three times that per hour. Compare the savings yourself.

Fan Clubs

Sex keeps your skin clear and rosy. A good cup of coffee can make a bad day tolerable. There's almost nothing that an afternoon and $70 spent in a bookstore won't fix. But it is also true that in affairs of aging, nothing helps the years fade away like your very own fan club.

"Yeah, right," I hear you snort. You're happy if you get a smile out of the dry-cleaning guy you've gone to for 10 years. How does plain, anonymous, almost-30 you go about surrounding yourself with slavishly admiring crowds? It's not hard, especially if you realize that it only takes two to form a club. Don't you remember anything from childhood?

A fan club, by definition, is any group devoted to the study, praise, and general well-being of another group or individual. Usually these fan clubs include a newsletter, sometimes even a convention, and, these days, a website. You can do any of this with just the two of you. Or hell, you could do it with just the one—you.

I had a girlfriend who often mused about publishing a 'zine, a sort of paper tribute to herself and her world views—which were decidedly wacky. She wanted to call it *Stacy's World*, and mostly she just wanted a venue for her Technicolor descriptions of dating hell and other aspects of life in New York as a single career chick. This was just a few years before 'zines started getting a lot of mainstream media attention and their creators tapped for lucrative mainstream media jobs. I wish she'd gone through with it, even if she'd only published one issue of *Stacy's World*. Stacy could put anyone in the hospital with her side-splitting retelling of "The Worst Date of My Life," and apart from having a fun way of working out her misery, she might have gotten a sitcom gig out of it as well.

Of course, a fan club doesn't have to involve anything as formal as an actual publication dedicated to your life and woes. It can take the form of you and your two closest friends making a pact to get together for dinner every Tuesday night in perpetuity. If the three of you enjoy each other's company, give a shit about each other's daily minutiae, and generally feel responsible for keeping each other's spirits up, it's a fan club.

Maybe I should have mentioned this before—along with the wrinkles and numerous new aches and pains, you will notice as you age an inability to tolerate other people's bullshit. This is particularly true when those other people happen to be "friends." You're too tired at the end of the day to waste time and energy on high-maintenance friendships that cause more grief than you feel you deserve. And because you're older and flush with newfound confidence, it's much easier to jettison this flotsam (or jetsam) than it would have been in, say, seventh grade when your list of best friends spanned two pages. It's better to admit the cold fact that you can count the number of real friends on one hand, rather than allowing it to slowly dawn on you one lonely fall weekend afternoon when everybody you know seems to be screening their calls.

Your fan club will help you weather all these ugly realities of life. Make sure you return the favor and be a dues-paying member of their fan clubs as well. How do you manage that? It's easy. Just stop thinking about your own misery for five minutes (this in itself is asking a lot) and do unto others. You must be willing to foot the cab fare from time to time. You must send them absurd gifts and a regular stream of postcards (my favorite: those "Hair Mail" postcards with fluorescent pink or leopard skin on one side and a space to write in on the other). You must not let long-distance rates keep you from regularly calling and checking up on the mental health of those in your fan club. Most importantly, you must give good career counsel when asked, never skimp on connections, and be brutally honest regarding all new haircuts.

Feeling Better? Did any of this help? I hope so. I really do. Because—and I really hate to bring you back to this point— you're about to turn 30 for real. But trust me, you'll be OK. So let's go on. You've read this far into the book, right?

6 THE GREAT BEYOND

Tan, Rested, and 30

Welcome to 30. Now you never have to go through that again.

A card received from a 33-year-old
girlfriend on my 30th birthday

Turning 30 is a lot like losing your virginity. You spend years working up to it, obsessing over it, fretting about what it will be like and how different your life is sure to be once it's happened—only to be left lying there afterward wondering when those fireworks you were supposed to see will start. "Is that it?" Indeed.

After what happened the weekend of my 30th birthday it's amazing I woke up on the big day itself at all. But I did and, surprise, I was still among the living. Moreover, I made a quick body check. Yep, everything was as I'd left it the night before, when I was still in my 20s. I checked the mirror for sudden new crevices in my face. There were none. That was good. Gingerly, I climbed out of bed and stood surveying the damage. Same old rented room. Same old student loan bills piling up in the same old bill box. Same old job I had to get to within the next hour. Only now I was 30. Me. Thirty years old. Hah. It was kind of funny, when you thought about it.

I'd never felt such relief in my life.

Now It Can Be Told

Assuming you've survived the whole dreadful turning-30 process, you're feeling, well, like a survivor, and pretty damn good to boot. After all, that which does not kill you only makes you stronger. In no instance is this more true than now.

Now you're 30. It's not so bad, is it? In fact, 30 suddenly seems a lot younger than it ever has before. Funny, that. It almost makes you understand why all the boomers are always bleating about this turning-50 business. (Except that now you'll have to endure your own parents droning on and on about how they can't believe they have a 30-year-old daughter.) Maybe there's something to that old saying "you're only as old as you feel." Hmm. You'll think about that.

The first thing you'll feel is relief. Soul-cleansing, slack-jawed relief. You will feel the sort of relief a doctoral candidate has when the one bastard on her thesis committee who hates her work is suddenly stricken with salmonella poisoning and must be replaced. Ever wormed your way out of a hellish school assignment? Ever somehow beaten an outrageous cab fare? Ever put your hand on the perfect holiday dress just minutes before the store closes—and it's on sale? That is how you will feel when you finally turn 30.

I was, in fact, feeling not just relief, but intense excitement. I now knew from personal experience that being 30 didn't look or feel any different than 29, 28, 27, even 26 (at 25 I was still a twit). In fact, I felt, oddly, stronger. I refuse to use the word *empowerment*, but that's kind of what it did feel like, as if I was finally ready to go out and do what needed to be done. I was young, yet experienced. I could go out and live my life on my terms. It felt good.

Not so very long after your 30th birthday, you will begin to see for yourself why being a chick in her early 30s is, in fact, the best place you've ever been to date. But first, take a deep breath, and tell me how you feel.

More substantial, maybe? (And I'm not talking about that pint of Häagen-Dazs you wolfed down last night, either.) A little more . . . worldly? It could very well be the power of suggestion at work on a large scale, but whatever. Go on and admit it. You're feeling the headiness of your years of experience already, and it's not a bad feeling at all. You sense that maybe people will start to take you a bit more seriously now that you're a little older. You're feeling a lot more certain of your own needs as well. Next time you want Thai food and your boyfriend wants pizza, you'll send him on his way and treat your Gold Card instead.

You're also looking damn good. Better, in fact, than you remember looking last year. There's something about confidence that is sexier than a little gold lamé dress, and most men (Hollywood execs and 14-year-old boys excepted) find it irresistible. It's a look that only comes when you've finally come to

The Ten Best Things About Turning 30

1. You'll never have to go through turning 30 again.

2. Everyone over the age of 30 still thinks you're a young snip of a girl.

3. You've got a whole new decade to work with—and this time you're prepared!

4. People will still envy you if you start a company or write an award-winning novel any time soon.

5. You start to sense that even if you never do either of these things, you can still have a productive, worthwhile, and happy life.

6. Grown-ups start taking you seriously. A good thing any way you look at it. If you still look like an artist, then you must be a serious artist. If you're a suit, venture capitalists may now allow you in the building.

7. That indomitable mop of curly hair or whatever other physical trait that so plagued you in junior high and high school is now your best feature.

8. Whereas in your 20s you insisted that you didn't give a damn what anybody else thought of you, now you *really* don't give a damn.

9. You're old enough to know better but young enough to do it anyway.

10. [Insert your own smart-ass reason here.]

terms with the body you have, the hair you can't change, and the face you deserve. Younger chicks can not replicate this look. Not until they've been where you've been, and done it, like you have.

The best part of all is, you have 10 years of this before you turn 40. "Turning 30 isn't about what you haven't done yet," insists Rosemary Ryan, the ad exec. "It's all about what you get to do now."

But I forget. Many of you out there are not yet 30, and so all of this helpful truth telling is like so much blather to you, and in fact, you're suddenly regarding this whole book rather suspiciously. If this is the case, the only thing I can suggest is to talk to a few chicks you know and admire who are already 30 or beyond and see what they have to say. I guarantee they will back me up on this one. Or hell, how about one more story about me, the turning-30 poster girl.

30 and Beyond

As bad as my 29th year was, my 30th made up for it. My 30th year was one of the best of my life. You know the outline—no deadlines, sexy Englishmen, free cigarettes, Greek food, Cypriot divers, Turkish bazaars, Tuscany villa . . . does that sound like a bad year to you?

Thirty-one was even better. I spent that birthday quietly by myself, house-sitting for some friends, smoking cigarette after cigarette on the deck of their lovely Craftsman-style house in a leafy New Jersey suburb. It was deep summer, less than a month after I'd returned from England to Newark without enough U.S. currency to even get the bus back to Manhattan. My leftover Turkish lire cashed out to something less than two cents U.S., and I was about ready to start panhandling for a quarter to call somebody (I don't know who) to come pick me up when two very kind chicks who'd overheard my tale of woe to the exchange clerk offered to give me the $6 bus fare. I almost started crying, and begged them to give me their mailing address so I could immediately return their money when I got into the city, but they refused and patted my back and wished me good luck as they blended back into the airport crowd. This, I thought, was good karma (and to this day I am ever vigilant for a stranded backpacker or two I can help out with an anonymous cash infusion). This incident had been the most trying event so far. Everything else was falling into my lap. When I finally arrived in New York, the first place I went was the *Business Week* offices in Midtown. As I schlepped uptown, cutting quite a metropolitan figure with my giant backpack and filthy hiking shorts, I realized what a home to me these offices had been the whole time I lived in New York. They were where I spent most of my Sundays. They were the last place I'd stopped at before leaving eight months earlier, and the first place I was going to grace upon returning. There had to be a grand metaphor in all that.

I was well past thin and a good way into emaciated by this time. I was also as tan as I'll ever be again. My urbane bob had long ago grown out and hung in streaked, straggly strands past my shoulders. I wore half a dozen cloth bracelets around my wrist, the mark of a traveler in certain circles, and still had two rubber bracelets from the kibbutz rubber factory dangling from my ankle. I hadn't worn makeup or earrings or deodorant for most of the year. As I rambled from office to office, saying hello to former colleagues, a small band of male editors gathered around me, smiling, like doting older brothers. When I left that day I had three freelance assignments, a job tip, and a couple of offers to house-sit. They actually wanted to see my pictures too.

But one look at the rental listings in the *Village Voice* took care of any notion I'd fostered about maybe staying in New York. Rents had gotten even more ridiculous, if that's possible, in the time I'd been away, and it was clear that to stay in this city meant I'd be a rent slave for the rest of my days. Such a lot was not for me. I preferred to spend two-thirds of my paycheck on rents in San Francisco, thank you, where at least the weather was a little better.

It was understood that one of the ramifications of quitting my job and traveling for most of the year was that I would have to return to the ancestral home. Normally this wouldn't have gone down well with me, since I hate going backward, but I really had no choice. And it gave me a chance to try out some of my newfound wisdom. Who cared how it looked, moving home at 31, I told myself. It'll be a good experience. Dad will take me out to sushi a lot. I'll only stay a month or two, get on my feet, and move back to San Francisco.

I spent five months, as it turns out, in the parental house, rebonding with family and savoring the languid, simple pace of a small southern California beach town. The first day back, my brother invited me out to watch him and some buddies surf. He'd never done that before, and as I sat watching them bobbing out past the break, waiting for the right wave, I wondered if this wasn't some larger sign designed to bring me back into the fold. I decided it was (I'm superstitious like that). Clearly I'd come full circle, I thought. So best to make the most of my time here.

Ventura is beautiful, which is good, because it has very little else going for it. It's a lot like Los Angeles must have been 40 years ago—there are still strawberry and lettuce fields all around, still undeveloped dunes and cracked, one-lane highways running parallel to miles of empty beach. The people who live there might work at the nearby Navy base or own a small business or pick vegetables or not work at all. My one brother owned a sign-painting business (most boats in the harbor sported his handiwork) and the other did construction. Both surfed religiously. Their friends' main worry in life was what *El Niño* was going to do to surf conditions in central California. They were all friendly. They didn't judge. They certainly didn't overachieve. But every last one of them seemed content with their lives. They knew what they were, and they didn't strive to be anything else. I could now, for the first time, see that they were perhaps on to something here. My youngest brother, in explaining his remedy for getting back into the swing of southern California, summed it up for me. "Jules," he said, "eat more burritos, and swim in the ocean."

Lots of burritos in San Francisco. Luke, of course, had never had one—not a proper one anyway. So that's what we had for dinner on the first night of his stay with me. Maybe I hoped cuisine would provide enough conversational fodder to keep us from talking about the real issue, which was us, and more specifically, just what the hell we thought we were doing.

We hadn't seen each other for six months, which slogged past in a blur of letters and once-a-week phone calls and my growing belief that he wasn't really going to make it to California. But here he was, on a tourist visa with one backpack full of stuff and nothing else. The big question of the moment was: could a kibbutz fling turn into a real relationship? Could we stand each other longer than two weeks at a time? Could we make it in the mundane world of rent, bills, work, and the occasional dinner out?

All that worrying for nothing. Within three weeks, when it became clear that I'd found the one straight man who knew the words to every Cole Porter song and wept during certain segments of *Fiddler on the Roof*, I dragged him down to city hall and married him. Immigration laws have a way of cutting to the romantic chase (i.e., we can't live together and both work so do we make it legal or not?).

Suddenly I was a married lady. At the time, we kept the news secret, and marveled at our own audacity. We broke the news to our parents a few weeks later. "I knew it," said my mom. A month later I got an interesting job that paid the rent and then some and Luke got his employment authorization card and two part-time jobs. We didn't have a lot of money (not with the rents in this town), and my student loan fiasco had come home to roost. But we were ridiculously happy. Things were on a huge upswing. Except that I couldn't shake an ongoing, queasy feeling in my stomach. I waited for it to develop into the flu, but it never did. Then I chalked it up to stress on the job, which there wasn't any of but it was the only explanation I could concoct. Soon I could no longer stomach the morning cup of coffee that had for the past 15 years been my lifeline to a full and productive day, and smoking no longer held the allure it had. By this time Luke was asking if I thought I could be pregnant. No way, I told him. I'd know if I were. And it's not like we were trying or anything.

I didn't believe it myself until I peed on the little stick and it turned pink. I swore to anyone who would listen that it wasn't intentional. Nobody believed me. But I took it as fate, as a sign. I was 31. Actually married. There was no way I wasn't going through with this. Luke was enthusiastic, and immediately took charge of overhauling my all-Cheerios diet. Wow. After years of sneering at pregnant ladies, now I was one of them. Who woulda thunk? I immediately ran out to buy the most obnoxious pair of clunky black clogs I could find to wear with my thrift-store black baby-doll/maternity dresses. No way I was going to look like a matron.

With these developments in place, life seemed much less a series of frustrations and more like, I dunno, room temperature butter, if you know what I mean. Luck, coincidence, and effort began converging more often, making life's little hassles seem less harsh. I started employing little lessons I'd learned in the last year as well. I stopped making the sorts of demands on myself that I had all during my 20s. I grew more patient. I started seeing patterns in both myself and in life in general that helped guide me (and that were probably there all along but I couldn't see them until now). I calmed down. I waited for things. I made little victories.

It was almost two years to the month that I realized in retrospect what had happened to me. The ladies at work had been right. My 30s were shaping up to be a far more kickass decade than my 20s. At 32 I had the contentedness and feeling of belonging I'd been looking for. I no longer felt compelled to prove anything to myself or anyone else. I could eat alone in a restaurant with nary a care. I could work a temp job without once dropping the name of my graduate school. The Buddhists must surely have a name for this state of mind. Maybe it's close to nirvana. Who knows?

Another incredible event happened when I was 32. I had my daughter! To date, she hands-down beats career, money, material goods, cool apartment, and cooperative hair (none of which I have anyway).

In one fell swoop this tiny girl took care of all my angst over higher purpose and meaning of life, and made me happier wiping strained squash off my T-shirt than I ever was chasing a byline. That notion would have gagged me at 22, but now, with a little life-experience at my back, my priorities have rearranged themselves. An unexpected byproduct is that I've suddenly become a grown-up—mostly because now I have someone to worry about besides myself—and I don't mind at all.

Three years ago I would have read an account like mine and responded with something appropriate like, "Well la-dee-fucking-dah. Goody for her." But I don't lay this saccharine ending on you just to gloat. I repeat it only because if it could happen to me, it can happen to any chick.

If you don't believe me, talk to any chick who's over 30. It just gets better from here.

Big, Juicy Rationales

Does all of this mean your terrors over the last five years about turning 30 have been for naught? Nay, they have not been for naught. It's a perfectly natural time in life to worry, and it's cosmically sanctified to boot. You have no reason to feel sheepish over your therapy bill or those really silly shoe purchases (you can't even get downstairs in those damn stilletos) over the last year.

Memorize these rationales and be prepared to whip them out whenever you need to. At a party, for example, an irritating little man tells you you're being silly feeling out of sorts over just another birthday, and that this just proves women are simply more emotional than men. Here you may use the line "*au contraire, mon frere,*" and proceed to drop one of the following on him.

The 30 Transition

The late Yale psychologist Daniel J. Levinson, whose bestselling *The Seasons of a Man's Life* was compiled from studies he conducted on the male life cycle, did a similar study on women, which was published just after he died in 1994. He interviewed 45 women at length about their lives between their early teens and mid-40s, and came up, not surprisingly, with a few chestnuts we can all know and love.

Levinson found that the early 30s are a "structure-changing or transitional period [that] terminates the existing life structure and creates the possibility for a new one." What that means is that the age of 30 is a natural and normal time in most women's lives to do a little adjusting, to figure out what went wrong and what went right up until now, and what it is that's really wanted anyway.

Joan Borysenko, Ph.D., wrote a whole chapter on this 30 transition in her very good, very worth-having-on-your-shelf book, *A Woman's Book of Life*, where she uses Levinson's study as a backdrop to this idea that 30 is a good and proper time to take stock of one's life. Levinson looked at two general groups of women, which for the sake of argument here we'll call the homemakers and the careerists. Both were coming up against the desire for change in their lives. By age 30, the women in the homemaking group were starting to get tired of home and hearth, of taking care of the kids and the husband and the dog, and were beginning to look at outside work or education as a way of gaining more confidence or independence. A lot of them got divorced in the years around their 30th birthday.

Two-thirds of the career women, on the other hand, weren't even married yet, having spent the bulk of their 20s getting educated, then building their careers. Many of them, Levinson reports, saw the age of 30 as a nudge to get going on finding a mate and starting a family before it was too late. For the more than half of the women in this group who were childless, married or not, the idea of starting to have kids became a significant source of stress.

So you see, we're not making any of this stuff up here.

The Seven-Year Itch

According to those wiser than we, a person's life can be divided up into seven-year cycles. There is one at 28 and another at 35. At every seven-year interval, the thinking goes, every cell in your body gets replaced. So it shouldn't shock you to hear that people undergo physical growth (during the first three cycles, anyway), mental growth, emotional growth, and other various and sundry upheavals. No sage worth his mountain retreat would ever brush off the notion of a gal going through a turning-30 crisis, because he'd know that such a transition is simply a normal part of the cycle of life. Anyway, the sages have written at length about this phenomenon, and who am I to poo-poo any of it?

Saturn Return

Check this out. There is actually an astrological reason for chicks to feel out of sorts around their 30th birthday, and it all has to do with the circles of the zodiac. Isn't that mysterious? Kelly Garton, 30, the ESL teacher and astrology student, calls it the Saturn Return.

The planet Saturn, in astrological terms, is the archetype of limitations. It takes 29 and a half years from your birth to circle the zodiac, and so for most people, it only comes around to have an impact twice in a lifetime. Three if you're lucky. Obviously the first time it returns packs a significant wallop. Saturn represents the physical limitations of what you can do, but another way of looking at it is representing what you've worked for and have accomplished for yourself thus far. "Not your dreams or luck, but things you can actually prove."

Depending on where Saturn was on the day of your birth is your own personal take on limitations (you're way over the top in all your endeavors, for example). You get a special reminder of this once every 30 years, when Saturn comes full circle. So no wonder, says Garton, that a lot of chicks (and OK, guys too . . . maybe) hit a wall around this age and start tearing their hair out wondering what it's all meant up till now, and what it is they really want to do with themselves. If you believe in this sort of thing, and a lot of people do, there isn't any big mystery as to why turning 30 is a milestone in life.

"Most people who watch this notice that it takes a couple years before and a couple years after to get things sorted out again," says Garton. Say, wouldn't this fit into the seven years between 28 and 35? See? It all connects! Synergy!

All right, so now you've got justification for feeling like your world was going to end just a short year or so ago. It wasn't so silly after all.

Clean Slate

I don't care what kind of vice you employed during your 20s. Maybe you were a drug-sodden slacker. Maybe you were a brazen yuppette. Maybe you fell somewhere in between. The beauty of turning 30 is now you have a nice, clean, fresh decade to work with. As one of the women who gave me the pep talk told me, "Your 30s are when everything finally clicks together." And you know how Americans love a clean slate (which probably explains the jump in bankruptcies). We love to roll up our sleeves, take a deep breath, and get to work. I know dozens of chicks who decided they were going to "reinvent" themselves in their 30s. They quit jobs and traveled, as I did. Or they quit jobs and started brand new ones in different fields. Or they finally got off the drugs. Or they finally got to run their division at work. Or they became mothers for the first time. The options are just endless, particularly since this is the first decade in which you're really sort of in control of your life.

Three Chunks

Need a better visual? Look at your life in three chunks. Making charts like this is not unlike making lists; it's just as silly but just as effective for seeing the bigger picture. To wit:

Age 0–10: Pretty much on automatic. You don't have much say in matters such as growth, what you eat, where you live, what you wear, or what your career choice will be, since most adults tend to smile and pat your head when you tell them you want to be either the Lone Ranger or a ballerina.

Age 10–20: Tumultuous years, these. Filled with traumas

such as first kisses, first periods, big zits, first heartbreaks, and the first time you can't get into a class you need to graduate. Did you really have all that much fun in this 10-year period?

Age 20–30: Life picks up a bit, but you're a bit fuzzy on what to do with yourself. You may have spent half this decade obediently pursuing something they told you to pursue. Or you may have spent it with your finger in your nose trying to figure out what to do with yourself. Either way, although you were gorgeously young and full of potential, you never seemed to have enough money or time to actually do something about it. One damn frustrating 10 years.

Age 30–whenever: Finally. You're starting to catch on to this life thing. You're finally comfortable with who you are and what you do best and the fact that you just can't wear those tube dresses the models wear. You choose how to grow, what to eat, where to live, and what to wear, and when you finally settle on a career, you've been around long enough to figure out how to do it. For example, you know they sell Lone Ranger masks down at the Walgreens.

Confidence Chick

Much has been written on what happens to girls when they hit adolescence. Up until puberty, girls, it seems, are identical to boys in ability and in spirit. They run, jump, dream, and spit as far as any kid in the clubhouse. But from the day they get it into their heads to start shaving their legs, girls' confidence levels begin to plunge. By the time the girl who'd beaten up every guy on her block hits 15, she's a gum-snapping girlie-girl who won't look anyone in the eye and who will defer to a boy every time. That sucks.

Stuff You Know That 22-Year-Olds Don't

✦ The company owes you dick.

✦ Not everyone has to like you.

✦ Nobody gives a damn about your college GPA.

✦ Stuff in and of itself won't make you happy.

✦ Some stuff you *need*, so you need to earn a decent living for yourself.

✦ Men are the frosting, but you are the cake.

✦ Your mom is probably on your side.

✦ When a guy insists it just isn't going to work, it isn't going to work.

✦ Suffering in the name of fashion is stupid and pointless. You'll need your Achilles tendon later in life.

✦ Thirty is actually pretty happening.

A gal can spend her entire 20s building the confidence it takes to climb back to where she was before she hit puberty and let guys, of all creatures, tell her how stupid she was. Through trial and error, through college and work and graduate school, a chick slowly learns that, actually, it's the men who are generally inferior and bent on macho games like chest-beating and war. She sees that she's just as smart and in almost all cases better at handling people than men are. She sees that men remain, at heart, little boys who can be easily toyed with, and she sees that no man is powerful enough to resist a wink of the eye, a turn of the leg, and a really well-made turkey sandwich.

When a gal turns 30, all the bravado she lost in junior high school comes back in a fierce way. Now she has the confidence and strength to look any man in the eye and spit. If she's too much of a lady to spit, she can get him to treat her to dinner.

What happened? It's simple; she has reached a higher level of chickdom. She possesses secrets, knowledge her younger sisters do not have. She knows when to stop drinking, she knows which DKNY items will go on sale next week and waits until then. She knows never to bother with any Barney's sale. She knows how to make extended long-distance calls at work that are utterly untraceable to her. She knows when to search her boyfriend's sock drawer and when it's just not worth it.

Think of yourself at 30 as Pippi Longstocking with a Gold Card. You do what you want and you have the means to do it.

There are other areas where you will improve as a chick now that you're no longer in your 20s. Specifically, these include your sex life and your career. Let's look at your career first because as much as you like sex you don't want to get screwed by your creditors.

7 IT'S JUST MY JOB

When the bell tolls and you find yourself suddenly in your 30s, remember that you are now allowed to cop a little attitude for yourself in your job. It's just one of the several hidden perks of joining the ranks of grown-ups.

After all, didn't you start out as an ill-paid, put-upon, glorified secretary, fresh out of college with your degree and your typing skills? Haven't you dutifully put in your time, making the coffee and fixing the copy machine for the idiots above you? Attending every damn fool meeting until the day one of the section managers looked up and took notice of you for seemingly the first time (maybe it was that blue dress?) and said, "You, you've been around for a while . . . what do you think?" And *voilà*, suddenly you were free to flash your brain brazenly for all to see. And they started coming to you more often with problems. And then you got a promotion. And a raise (and about time too). You got vested, or you finally got those stock options that are going to buy you a house next year. And by the time you're nearing 30 you suddenly realize that you can fulfill those five-year-minimum-experience requirements on all new job postings that used to vex you in your early 20s. You realize you're pretty good at what you do and, more surprising, other people think so too. An amazing development. Managers ask for your take on things routinely now, and they genuinely seem to listen and sometimes you shock yourself with the amount you actually know and the bravura with which you can decant it. You start noticing how young the entry-level chicks look these days, so young you don't think you could trust them to file a report for you—until one ventures up and asks if she can pick your brain about how you got to where you are today.

Where you are today. Ah. Sounds pretty great, no? It's heady stuff to suddenly find yourself a competent professional. It makes you feel almost like you're not just pretending to be a real grown-up. It almost takes the sting out of aging.

Ask any woman who's way into her career and she'll tell you the same thing: the 30s are when people finally start taking you seriously as a professional. You start to benefit from experience, know-how, confidence, and sheer seat-time no matter what industry you're in. These are good things, all.

Yes, but. What every chick will figure out sooner or later is that this experience thing has two faces. Along with all the good things like respect, position, and possible financial splendors comes the understanding of how things in the workaday world really work. Or let me put it this way: how things *still* work, at the end of the 20th century, a good 30 years after man allowed woman to start evolving out of the primordial typing pool.

A Cautionary Tale

Chicks worldwide should pity Jamie Tarses. Not because she was a highly paid, highly placed woman in Hollywood, but because the powers-that-be in her industry set her up to take the bullet for an ailing network, and figured they could because she was a 33-year-old chick. Tarses was only 32 years old when ABC tapped her to join its network as president of the entertainment division. Wonks everywhere gasped. Such a *young* woman to head a major network was unprecedented (no matter that there are lots of examples of boys that young running things). How would she manage the politics of Hollywood with so little experience to draw from? Could she be a leader people would follow? Not a year later, Tarses was publicly usurped and stripped of much of her actual power when they brought in a man—not too much older either—to oversee her work. An article written by reporter Lynn Hirschberg in the *New York Times Magazine* became the talk of the town on both coasts, pointing out what would be fairly obvious to any chick who's ever worked in corporate America, but was apparently news to everyone else—that Tarses had been set up all along to take the fall. In the piece, Hirschberg quoted agents and others in the industry as saying Tarses was simply too green to take the job. Too inexperienced. Too much a girl. One colleague (who for obvious reasons asked to remain anonymous) said dealing with her was like dealing with a girlfriend. He was almost afraid to break hard news to her, he said, because she might start to cry.

Count to 10. Deep breath. Continue.

I followed the Tarses drama from the time I first read about her ascending to the job at ABC to her undoing the next year because I too was agog that someone my age could be tapped to run a network entertainment division. Of course I thought she'd make a great profile for this very book, and of course I tried for about a month to get her to call me back, even to decline. But when she didn't, how mad could I be? After all, I reasoned, "This chick's *busy!*" So busy she probably never noticed that her 30th birthday had come and gone.

But her dramatic fall from grace pissed me off. Even though I already think Hollywood is run by a bunch of repressed Ivy League boy-men, and even though Tarses and I likely have nothing in common apart from our age and the fact that we both grew up in Los Angeles, and even though I'd certainly be too scared to say anything to her even if she did call me back, I still felt for her. She's a perfect example, whether she knows it or not, of how there's still a double standard in effect with regard to women, their jobs, and aging.

As Tarses found out, too many men still see women in their early 30s as girls. No matter how talented they are, no matter what kind of fresh ideas they may bring to the job, they are second-guessed to death. A woman in a demanding job is not treated in the same manner as a man the same age.

Knowing this instinctively, a chick might venture to ask why it is nobody ever referred to Bill Gates as a mere snip of a boy when he was steering the Microsoft leviathan in his early 30s. Or why didn't the media look to Michael Dell, who founded Dell Computer as a teenager and jump-started the mail-order computer industry in his 20s, and cite his boyish tomfoolery every time his stock prices dropped? Questions such as these are, alas, largely rhetorical, as any chick who's worked for a living knows. And that is because, even at the end of the millenium, men still run the show in the world of work.

I can happily report, however, that Michael Dell did throw a male friend of mine into his own turning-30 hell. This buddy, a journalist in his late 20s, gloomily told me how during a lull in his interview with Michael Dell, they looked at each other and realized they were the same age. "It was horrible," my friend moaned afterward. "He's a ba-jillionaire, and I'm . . . not."

"And you're never gonna be if you stay in journalism," I reassured him.

It's Kind of a Living . . .

It's important to understand what happened to Jamie Tarses because as a chick reaches her 30s and starts enjoying what her years of experience have reaped her, she needs to memorize this phrase: it's all qualified.

It is the end of the 20th century and women still earn 70 cents for every dollar a comparably qualified man makes. A whole generation of chicks have grown up with as much or more education as men and this is still the case. Almost every trade publication publishes a "Who Makes What" of their industries once a year, and every year it reveals that—surprise!—the workers with penises earn more. This happens in every single industry, with the possible exception of those six or seven women who are beautiful enough to make millions on their bone structure and only go by their first names. Likewise, the articles surveying the 100 top-paid executives in America read like an all-male revue. (All white too, natch.) You need sunglasses and a testosterone-counter as well if you open any major corporation's annual report and view the mugs of its directors. Yeah, yeah, there's always one, perhaps two female members, maybe even a dash of color on a few of the more enlightened (or politically correct) boards. But in general it's still 1970 in corporate America.

These are facts. Published in black and white, all the time, year-round.

So it is with this information stuffed firmly in cheek that we women have to proceed with the career building. Now we can be taken more seriously—as long as we don't get out of hand and reach too high. Although many a chick has proven that she can go as high as she wants as long as she wants, most of these would have to admit that to do so means beating the boys at a game of their own design.

A good many young women start getting this hint around about the time they've put in a good seven or eight years on the job. It sinks in slowly, especially to our generation, who grew up under the goodwill of the women's movement but with none of the understanding of what it was like for women before. We grew up with unlimited options. It never once occurred to us that we couldn't be math professors or nuclear scientists or plumbers if that's what we wanted to be. And it took a few years out of college or trade school to start seeing examples of how wrong we were.

I remember the first time I found out that a male colleague with exactly the same degrees and exactly the number of years of experience made a good $20,000 more a year than I did. It had to be a mistake, I figured. An oversight in human resources. I boldly went to a boss and asked, and came up for the first time against the sorts of rationales the guys in charge come up with to justify this sort of thing.

"He's done this job before." (A lateral move is good?)

"He's in a more specialized area."

"He came in at a higher level. You started as an intern."
(Silly me.)

And my all time favorite: "What have you done to deserve
such a pay raise?"

OK. So I'm bitter. I'm probably not the best person to talk
to about career mobility since I'm pretty much unfit for corporate employment anyway. Annual reviews alone make me want
to quit immediately and run screaming from the building (and
you should see how I act *after* the review). I can't get the
wardrobe down, combining $200 dresses with comfy black
clogs and no makeup may work for Sandra Bullock but not for
me. Nor have I ever been able to stomach holding the same
job for more than three years, falling into complete, demoral-
ized slave mode by the middle of the second year, so that by the
end of the third, I am almost completely unproductive and surly
and prone to walking around with my head in my hands,
moaning that there's no hope, no hope. So you see, I'm forced
to write because I'm not competent to do anything else. Which
also means I spend a good part of my year temping so I can
ensure shelter from month to month. In another era I would
probably sell matchsticks.

Talk instead to the millions of women out there who've
managed to go quite far and do quite well for themselves in
their careers. But they will also tell you that their victories are
based on the male pattern of success, and that money and corporate glories just ain't what we were led to believe back when
they told us we could now have it all.

Silicon Implant

Linda Sandifer is a 40-year-old financial consultant in Sunnyvale, California who hasn't exactly gone unrewarded for her years of hard work and her skills. While not one of the rare female millionaires Silicon Valley has minted in the last 20 years, she has enough money to live comfortably in her affluent surroundings and at the same time finance her fine art collecting and design avocations.

Sandifer came of age in the mid-70s, when Watergate and the women's movement were both in full fury. People were challenging authority in every arena, and when she entered college to study accounting, there was not a doubt in her mind that she would rise to the top of her profession.

"I bought into the career thing lock, stock, and barrel. I really thought that women had 'settled' by having kids. And I thought you could get all of your fulfillment in life by being dedicated to your career," she says. "It was really just a pendulum swing from the other extreme."

Her mother, she thinks, was not happy with her sole option of getting married and having children. She would much rather have been a career woman, which to her meant not just a successful teacher or successful nurse, but a woman who made lots of money. Sandifer grew up with that notion.

She went the financial route, studying accounting at the University of Maryland, where she met her husband, John, a software engineer. Hearing the call of high-tech, the two relocated to San Francisco in the early '80s, just in time for the personal computer revolution.

Sandifer thrived on the Valley's hard-work, hard-play culture. Her professional life consumed her time, rewarded her personally and financially, and kept her challenged through the cutthroat, fast-paced world of Silicon Valley finances.

She was in her early 30s by the time she looked up and assessed her situation.

"I think it was when I was working for a company where I worked for the CFO direct. Here was a guy just a couple years older than me. I'd always thought I'd be a CFO, but when I saw the toll it took on him, I saw what it took from him to be that way, and it just disgusted me. It was a turnoff. I thought, this isn't what I want to be."

She'd had enough. She'd done all of the "right" things to get to where she'd gotten, and she didn't like the thought of continuing to do those same things to keep progressing. She was losing her stomach for Valley politics and its consumer culture as well. "Still driving a Honda?" from an acquaintance looking down at her from his new Lexus was just the kind of attitude she, who could afford any car she wanted, couldn't take anymore. She wanted to have more control over her work and her life.

"I'd always worked my life around the job," she said. "I couldn't just take a vacation. I always had to plan it around a quarter-end audit, or a year-end audit, or whether the numbers were being released that week. There were always external things related to the company that determined what I could or couldn't do."

It was about this time that a lot of her friends started having babies. She regarded this trend with disdain. Clearly there were some women who just didn't have what it took to soar in their careers, she thought. The idea of having kids had been a timing problem for her in the past. "Somewhere in my late 20s there was this biological, cellular urge to have kids, and my husband, John, wasn't ready for it," she said. "So it just got tabled. Because I knew early on that if I ever did decide to have kids, I had to have a man who really wanted them."

There came a point in her early 30s that she was questioning her motivations and expectations for herself. She looked at the two options in front of her and asked herself what she was afraid of.

"I wondered why I thought I'd be a failure if I had a child," she recalls. "All these other women around me were having kids and they didn't see it as being failures at all, they saw it as being empowered."

That's when she realized for the first time that there was a male model of success and a female model of success, and that it was the male model she'd been patterning herself after all these years: an all-consuming career, an overshadowed family life.

By the time she saw that she could have a family and work that she loved, she'd lost interest. "Instead of giving my all to the corporation, I'd have to give my all to this child. And at this point I don't want to do any of that, I just want to give my all to myself."

Which she does. A few years ago she left corporate America and went out on her own as a financial consultant. Such work brings her the challenges of working in a variety of different fields as well as financial rewards. As she grows her business, she's slowly laying the groundwork for a venture she's always dreamed of operating: import textiles. Looking back over her career, she doesn't regret her choices, but she wishes she could have seen things more clearly for what they were in the beginning. But that's youth for you.

"To really be happy, you have to have a balanced life, and that means having friends and family and work that you love.

Anyone who's looking for it to be any one thing is probably going to be disappointed.

"You can't have it all," she says. "Not at the same time. Not unless you're really very wealthy and can afford the best full-time child care."

Filling the Suit

Some power-career chicks are happy—nay, relieved—to turn 30 because it means they can finally fill their Armani suits.

It wasn't so much the physical aging that worried Rosemary Ryan. She readily admits that with her power suits and professional demeanor, people have been mistaking her for 35 for years. "I remember getting hired by Chiat Day at 26, and my boss said, 'You're young, but you carry yourself like you're 30, so you'll be fine.'"

It was more a matter of perception—how she perceived herself and how those around her perceived her. She was used to being the bright young thing on Madison Avenue, the ingenue with the creativity and astute business savvy of someone far older. Now, she worried, people might be bored with her. She might wow her colleagues at 29, but at 30, her observations or ideas might be seen as merely competent work from a mature professional. "I really worried that people's perceptions of me could change in the space of a day."

It took about a year before she finally started feeling at ease with her new decade. And she noticed it, of all places, in the shower. "I remember that shower," she laughs. "I looked down at myself and I thought, 'My God, I'm a woman. I'm not a girl anymore. And it felt tremendously comfortable because I didn't always feel comfortable being young. Sometimes, I absolutely felt like a kid at the grown-up table."

So being the kid wonder sometimes had its pitfalls? "It did," she admits. There were times when she'd avoid confessing her real age simply so she could avoid the typical response: a gasp from a client, perhaps even a flicker of doubt that someone so young could handle so large an account.

But in her 30s she soon realized the upside. Peers still regarded her as a young hot-shot, but they also paid her the respect someone with her talent and experience deserved. This new combination suited her well. Indeed, the more she thought about it, the more she realized that she'd finally grown into her real age. "I was born 35," she laughs. "I was never one to be a rebel as a kid. I was very independent, and I didn't need a lot of supervision. So now I find I'm really comfortable in this skin."

Temp Nation

Cynthia Baker was a temp. By her own reckoning, she has had almost 100 assignments from the time she graduated college at 23 to recently, when she turned 33. This condition sprang, she figures, from her choice of major—psychology—and her ability to type. "I knew enough about psychology to know I should have had my head examined for being a temp for so long," she says. But this L.A. woman got hip to a better plan after figuring out she could combine what she knew about office management with what she knew about human nature. She now sells her time to start-ups who need intuitive database and administrative schemes set up fast. She is very good at what she does, and, after a shaky three months in the beginning, very in demand. Getting even 40 minutes of her time over the phone took three weeks of telephone tag. She's well paid, she's well respected, she's well dressed. Can you guess what she does? (Hint: she's not a temp anymore.)

A good 40 percent of the workforce (or more, depending on when you're reading this) are temporary employees. It's a clever way corporate America has devised to avoid any obligation to those members of its workforce that it can't relocate to the Third World. Chances are you've been a temp at one time or another yourself, so you know the spiel: short-term assignment, low hourly wage, no benefits, no sick pay, no vacations, and the vague promise of a staff job kept in front of you like a carrot on a stick. If you're the kind of gal who prefers a life to a job, as we discussed in an earlier chapter, then temping might be the ideal gig for you: easy work, no commitment, office politics that never stick to your veneer. But by the time you're nearing 30, your taste for eight hours of filing at $9 an hour may be waning. You may suddenly want to be honest about what it is you do for a living. You may be chafing at certain Temp Nation rules like the one that says all girl temps must be admins who never make more than $15 an hour, while boy temps are computer experts making $20 an hour and up. Or you may simply have had as much bullshit as you can take and now want revenge.

If you find yourself in this situation, come closer. Let me whisper one word in your ear: consulting.

"What?" you gasp, shocked at my insolence. You're not qualified to be a well-paid consultant? Poppycock. Anyone can be a consultant. It's true that there are "real" consultants with experience in scary subjects like finance, manufacturing, and UNIX, but it is also true that the world is full of 22-year-old consultants pulling down the big bucks telling middle managers with 20 years of experience how to reorganize their flowcharts.

Much more important than experience in the world of consulting is confidence. No, scratch that. You need more than confidence, you need *bravado*. Big, swinging-dick bravado. You need to convince yourself, and just one project manager, that you've got a skill his group can't do without, and that you are the only qualified person in this hemisphere to do it. You will need all this bravado because you must be able to look him in the eye and get him to pay you $50 an hour to set up and maintain his database when not two weeks ago, you were a $13-an-hour temp doing the same thing at another company. And you've got to make this guy think he's done the best thing for his group as possible by hiring little old you.

Why are your knees quaking? Men do this all the time. The only difference between them and you is that they've got the slight advantage of built-in testosterone that makes it easier for them to believe they're worth $75 an hour. Believe me, sister, you're worth more. But your fee will increase steadily after every assignment, won't it? If it will help any, use this plan as an excuse to go out and buy yourself a really kick-ass black wool power suit and practice your swinging-dick bravado at home in the mirror.

I believe that any chick who's spent the last 10 years earning a living has had her rose-tinted glasses stomped on by the Doc Martin of reality. The workaday world is not fair or fun or particularly friendly, and it certainly doesn't give a damn about you or your ideals. But a girl's gotta earn a buck somehow. The bottom line for the 30-ish chick building her career is this: win the game any way you want, but win it for yourself.

8 DATING IN YOUR 30s

May I be crass and point out the obvious? If you're not married by now, you've probably been dating longer than most marriages last. You possess certain knowledge; perhaps you've even deciphered a page or two from *The Secret Guy Decoder Book* (and I applaud you if you have). You've studied men for years now. You know they're a strange breed, very unlike the superior female of the species. At this point, you know what you want in a date. And it's probably not a lot like what you wanted in a date when you were 20. You have probably also figured out that dating in your 30s is a different animal entirely. No longer that pink-nosed, fuzzy-tailed, hopeful little lamb it was in your tender years. No, now it is something more akin to a tarantula. *Eew!* How gross, you say. And I agree. But let me explain.

No Rules

When an editor girlfriend of mine first told me about the book *The Rules* and what was contained therein, I was repulsed yet fascinated, much like craning your neck to see the bloody car accident while loudly protesting that you hate rubberneckers. (This book promises to yield time-tested methods for finding a husband, provided you turn yourself into a southern society sister circa 1955.) You may have heard about this book yourself, and God forbid, perhaps you even picked it up (as a cultural/sociological experiment, I *know*) to peruse the information within. I'm sure you were immediately overcome with a need to ingest some purifying matter and ran to the fiction section to read through some Melville until you felt better. I'm sorry for this experience, but I wasn't there to snatch the book from your hands and throw it into a safe area, like near the bodice busters.

This is not *The Rules*. Please. It is my opinion that any man snared in that way is not worth snaring except maybe to show off to your friends as an amusing curiosity before letting him loose again. Despite appearances to the contrary, there are good guys out there who will love you without your makeup on. Guys who are thrilled that you called them back and asked them out. Guys who will be patting themselves on the back for having met such a boffo, independent-minded, nongame-playing, sexy-ass chick like yourself. Never fall into the desperation trap.

Places to Meet Men

The chick in her 30s who still insists on meeting guys in bars has told herself that she really wants the kind of guy you meet in bars. She deserves what she gets. By the time you are 30 you have probably gleaned that guys met in bars aren't the sort of upright (standing, I mean), sentient men the average girl considers husband material and you have moved on. But by now you have skipped down many of the more obvious roads in search of love—Blind Date Blvd., Workmate Way, Aunt Aggie Ave.—and none have gotten you where you want to be. Clearly, more creative methods need to be employed. I recommend signing up for a swing dancing class right this instant.

I know what you're thinking. You're thinking, "But I took five ballroom dancing classes over the course of my 20s, and the only guys I ever met were balding 45-year-olds named Norm." I know. I myself have an adventure-in-ballroom-dancing episode to relate (of course). My girlfriend Eva and I signed up for a ballroom dancing series at the local community center. There we were after work, dancing away, having a good time with the other ladies and pleasant if otherwise unremarkable men, when it happened. He came in 20 minutes into the class, the 5-foot-tall man with a high red afro, polyester shirt, gold chains, and an Eastern European accent. He surveyed the room. Every woman in the place looked down at her feet. Of course he made a beeline for my friend, who stared at me and mouthed "Help," as he asked her for the next dance. For the rest of the evening he followed her around, and at the end of the night demanded her number, even though we told him she wasn't from this country, lived with her father and six brothers, and in fact didn't own a phone.

Swing dancing doesn't attract these types. For one thing, a "one-armed pretzel turn" is a lot harder and takes far more coordination than a four-step cha-cha. Many of the jumps and swings require strength, and leading demands a certain height requirement. There also seem to be laws of etiquette inherent to the swing set, which hearken back to the good old days when men wore fedoras and lit a gal's cigarette. If you don't mind being called a "tomato" (and I think it's charming), you just may meet the man of your dreams. At the very least you'll meet guys who can dance better than you and have a keen sense of style. You may even learn how to make a decent martini, which may help you pay your rent one day.

Matchmakers

Professional matchmakers are to the '90s what computer dating was to the '80s. Let's hope it works a little better than the abominations formed when two people got matched according to their birth date, eye color, favorite food, and zip code. At least in matchmaking, there's an actual person involved. And there's significant historical precedent as well.

Matchmakers can also be expensive. But if you are now in a position to afford such services, you should avail yourself of them. The pool of guys is generally of a higher quality than ordinary guys off the street. And these kinds of services cut through to the chase quite handily. You and the man you meet (who has also paid for the service) presumably share the same romance objective.

Do-Gooder Events

Get a girlfriend. Sign up for the March of Dimes walkathon. Or the AIDS danceathon. Or volunteer to man a booth at the local street fair. All of these options put you in the midst of hundreds, sometimes thousands, of members of the opposite sex of varying eligibility.

All right, it's true that the AIDS danceathon may net you a lot of really hot men (if you dance really well), but few of them will be willing to sleep with you. No matter! Gay men are always ready, willing, and able to help out when it comes to hair, body, and makeup tips. I suggest you avail yourself of their services, as they probably know more about these things than you do.

Otherwise, however, have a good time at those do-gooder events. You will thank me because you will look up one hot July afternoon, as you man some nonprofit's chili dog booth, and you will notice that you are surrounded by admiring men. They may be admiring your community spirit (or they may be admiring your sweaty, clingy T-shirt). Either way, the situation affords them a wholesome, easy way to strike up a conversation with you, and you with them. As much as half an hour can be spent prattling about matters other than the matter at hand, which is, of course, your relationship status, your phone number, whether you like Indian food, and so on.

How to Survive an Evening with Three Couples

An unfortunate by-product of getting older is that everyone around you starts to pair off. This means the likelihood of your spending an entire night with couples who want to talk about their engagement rings and new couches is growing ever larger. Typically, there is a grace period of a year or two when you still have a single girlfriend or three who can be relied upon for social succor. But one day you may well find yourself the last little girl in the singles box of your college alumni magazine. And if you want to leave your apartment at all, it will mean having to spend an evening with at least one couple, and, in the worst-case scenario, two or more newly formed couples. In New York,

I had one girlfriend who returned from just such a night and forced me to take a cab across town to sit with her all night on a suicide watch. It shook her up bad. "They all talked about engagement rings!" she wailed. "They didn't even want to eat!"

These can be trying times. But here are some guerrilla tactics for getting out of these situations when you find yourself in them:

- Call your drop-dead gorgeous gay friend and beg him to take pity on your wretched soul by accompanying you on this evening and act butch enough to pass. Tell him he will not have to kiss you, and that you will pay for all food and drinks. Throw in an introduction to your hunky brother if he balks.

- Arrive with a tasteful carry-on bag and wait until the conversation turns to in-laws or some equally depressing topic then jump up with a flurry and exclaim that you're so sorry to miss out on the rest of the evening but you have a flight to catch to Paris. Quickly explain that it's just a little spur-of-the-moment trip and Renaldo bought you the tickets. Smile mysteriously but say nothing when asked who Renaldo is. Remember to wave your hand absentmindedly when you next see any of these couples and they ask you again who this Renaldo is, as if he were just so much last-month's news. They will feel very settled and boring in comparison to you.

- Announce that you've taken up a new religion that advocates free love and hearty group sex among its members, all between the ages of 19 and 35, and that you now enjoy the attentions of several handsome young bucks. But tragically, there are three females for every male, and you must find some new recruits. Would your friends be able to suggest anybody?

Central Dating Dilemma for Chicks in Their 30s

Guys are mostly dorks. Far too many of them, or at least most of those still left on the singles scene, appear to have delusions of grandeur, and believe that although they're short, balding, and still living at home with Mother, they will only date 19-year-old foreign exchange students.

But this is an established fact. The central dating dilemma for a girl who is almost 30 is the guy-promoted idea that since she is almost 30 she wants to be married yesterday. Many guys believe that marriage is suddenly the sole reason for dating, and if they are to remain roving, independent guys, they must date only chicks who are too young to pressure them about marriage, must less spell it.

As we know, this idea of women as fixated on marriage is a myth. And one that should have died out in 1972. But it lingers still. And so what if some of us do long to meet a nice guy (or in some states, a nice gal) with whom we can settle down? It's only a matter of survival, and it benefits both parties by getting them out of the singles scene and enabling them to afford a decent one-bedroom apartment.

Besides, although we all want to meet Mr. Right, we can pass if it's at the expense of our own happiness. We, unlike unmarried chicks of yesteryear, do not need to be married, because we have good jobs, education, and lots of attitude. We can take care of ourselves in perpetuity, thank you very much.

And even though there are still a few chicks out there who have the idea that they need to get married for financial security, they are usually off the market early on. If you're into octogenarian millionaires, don't let me stand in your way. Just don't sign that prenup.

Men are very attached to their unattachment. It's an inborn trait with them. Many spook and bolt at the first sign of real commitment. It's a tiresome male quirk, but you, a chick in your 30s, know what to do next.

Say you meet a guy and he seems like a winner during that all-critical first month: he called you promptly, for example, after you let him spend the night after the third date; your girl-friends have given him an enthusiastic thumbs-up; his hygiene continues to be good. You should know by now that what comes next is the critical juncture. It could take as little as a small card, sent to him as a token of your affection and friendship, to alarm him into canceling your next date. Other things trigger it as well. One phone call too many, despite how important the information you have to relate to him is. The rhetorical question "What are we doing?" posed while lying in each other's arms. You're barely aware you've said it, such bliss you're in. But to him, it's the beginning of the "relationship talk," and hence the beginning of the end.

What do you do? I say, to hell with all the games. Make another notch on your bedpost and walk away from the whole mess. The weevil will either sink back into the woodwork—in which case you made the correct assumptions about his character and you are better off without him—or he will realize two weeks later that you are the woman for him and come crawling back, at which point you know what to do. I don't have to lecture a chick your age on how to make a guy beg.

Men Who Love Their 30-Year-Old Chicks and the Way We Reward Them

There are men out there, and lots of them, who think that women in their 30s are the sexiest things since the WonderBra. "I think a woman who's 30 is much more interesting," says Dan LaSalle, 28. "They're much more . . . knowing."

These are the kind of enlightened men you want to sink your teeth into. But there is a definite supply-and-demand problem. My suggestion is to find men in their early to mid-20s, who are apt to be awed with your character, experience, and sexual drive, and will be your willing love slave for years to come. Men in this age group are not experiencing any turning-30-related anxieties themselves that might adversely affect a relationship.

Personal Ads

Now might be the time for you to explore your very first personal ad. For many a chick, reading the personal ads has heretofore been regarded as an evening's entertainment, perused for a laugh over coffee with the girls. ("Hey, listen to this one: 'Portly middle manager seeks virgin, 18–21, for fire sacrifices and walks on the beach. Must like animals and have sense of humor.'") For one thing, it may very well have taken 15 years of dating before you could articulate in words just what it is you're looking for.

I'm told these things actually work. I'd be more dubious, because the one ad I actually ventured to answer never reaped a reply of any kind, shaming me into never doing such a thing again. ("He must have hated my picture! What was I thinking?") But I do have a very good girlfriend who met a man she dated seriously for two years from a personal ad. She might have married him, too, except that the further he got along on his psychology doctorate the weirder he got, until almost anything she uttered—"Pass the ketchup, please," for example— became cause for a lecture on her dominating nature. She was forced to move on.

Then again, the one other likely candidate she met through this method took her out on a fabulous date in which the chemistry and the wine flowed, set up a second date, and then left a message on her answering machine telling her it was probably a waste of time so he was canceling, but good luck in the future. I guess this goes to show that it's a crapshoot out there.

Still, it's one option that, if you're adventurous and have a good sense of humor, just might reap results.

What to say in a classified ad? This depends on what you're looking for. Husband? Someone to eat sushi with you? Someone to eat sushi *on* you? Craft your ad appropriately. Start by studying the ads in whatever publication you're thinking about placing an ad in and go from there. It also helps to realize the basic difference between the kind of ads men write (they all require photographs) and those women write (they're all looking for commitment). Avoid the urge to play with a guy's mind by sending along a picture of Cindy Crawford. Avoid leaving nasty-grams on the machines of those pathetic men who are over 40 but want to date "girls" in the 18-to-21-year range. Please try to have a smidge of originality and think of things you enjoy doing other than candlelight dinners, the outdoors, and walks on the beach (even if those are things you do enjoy). Think of three other things you really enjoy that stand out from the crowd: dwarf bowling, macrobiotic sushi, and film noir. Now I might answer an ad like that.

Beware of being too self-aware in your ad, however. By the time a gal is 30, she can sum up who she is and what she wants in a couple of deftly written lines. Men, however, might be confused by the result. Kelly Garton tried a personal ad recently. She wrote:

> Do you love god? Are you compassionate, raunchy, offbeat, love beauty? Are you as comfortable at a church convention as at a dance concert or on a train in a distant country? I'm 30. Call me.

If you remember, Kelly is a very interesting chick who spent her 20s teaching English in far-flung locales. She's also an astrology student, very spiritual and open, and happens to be a dancer as well. "I figured if they didn't understand that last phrase they wouldn't call at all," she says. And she was right. She got a total of five calls, and in retrospect, she would have toned down the God part. "I got a couple of calls from guys with God issues."

A better ad, aimed at your typical male, might have read like this:

> Dark-haired beauty. Slim, muscular, good rhythm. Seeks soul mate. I want to read your chart tonight.

Mr. Right and Mr. Right Now

By now you know that Mr. Right only comes along every third leap year, and when he does, he is just as likely to be in Uzbekistan as where you are. Still, we need to know the difference between Mr. Right and Mr. Right Now.

Mr. Right Now is the temporary fix. He's your methadone. He'll get you through a dry spell. He's the guy you go to the movies with because you actually washed your hair this morning. Mr. Right Now is the guy you screw but genuinely don't want to know anything more about him than that he wears Ralph Lauren boxer briefs. He is the guy you apologize to your friends about. He is a stopgap measure.

And Mr. Right? Defining Mr. Right is like defining obscenity: you'll know it when you see it, although a good bet is any guy who buys you Pop Tarts without you ever asking for them.

Nice Jewish Boys

In the husband-material category, Jewish men rank high. Jewish men are often smart, funny, handsome, ambitious, and/or socially conscious and make good family types when the kids come. It is lesser known (but a distinct selling point) that they are generally pretty good in bed too. Many single chicks agree you could do a lot worse than finding yourself a nice Jewish boy to date.

But try to find one. A good friend of mine and I once stayed quite late after work yabbering away about this very topic: the likelihood of meeting and marrying a nice Jewish man. We determined, after much discussion, that we were statistically more likely to win the $100 million Lotto jackpot on numbers we'd made up while stoned.

Here is our reasoning: by the time the nice Jewish man is in his mid-30s, or prime marrying age, he is likely already married, or, if not, seriously flawed. If he is the same age as you he will want someone younger. If you aren't Jewish he may fall madly in love with you, but only because he has the convenient out of saying he can't marry you because you aren't one of the tribe. If you are Jewish, he will dump you for a *shiksa*, preferably an Asian woman. When nice Jewish boys turn 40 they suddenly realize they do want marriage and family after all and so rush out and meet nice 25-year-old Jewish girls. (Or if they're Jerry Seinfeld, nice Jewish 18-year-olds.)

If you're a chick in your 30s and would like to marry a nice Jewish boy, the odds are, unfortunately, against you. You really can't win in this instance, we decided. So don't even bother trying. No wonder intermarriage rates are so high. Oy.

Guys and Shoes—A Connection?

Whether or not you want to get married, by the time you're in your 30s, what you want most of all is simply a guy who will fit your lifestyle and your budget. I liken this desire to looking for the perfect pair of shoes.

I'm not Imelda Marcos (only because I don't have her closet space), but bear with the metaphor, won't you? Shopping for shoes. You go in with some idea of what you're looking for, find the section that has the shoes you like best, at a price you can afford, and, with economy of time in mind, you commence trying them on. Some pairs you would never consider picking up at all. Some don't fit. Others fit fine, but make your legs look too stocky. Still others seem perfect at first, but need to be returned in a week because they give you blisters. You'll know when you've found the perfect pair of shoes. They're likely to be the ones you might not have tried on were it not for the prodding of a girlfriend. You know it from the start, the

Dating Tips from Those Who Know

These are handy hints from a gaggle of genuine single chicks in their early 30s who have been there, done that, and don't plan on doing it again, unless, of course, we're talking about Mr. Right here.

✦ Do not move across country for a guy unless you're 100 percent sure he's the one. In fact, ask yourself why this guy can't move across the country for you.

✦ Agree to blind date. Even though most are disastrous, they can be entertaining if you take the right attitude. It's a documented fact that many chicks have met their husbands on blind dates, so you just never know. Besides, you're getting a free dinner, what are you complaining about?

✦ Never think for a minute that you might be able to get back together with your old boyfriend, the one you lived with after college and who broke your heart. This never works and never has in the history of mankind. Even if he's single at the moment, don't go there.

✦ Remember the rule of three. Give a guy three chances to

moment you put them on, that these are the shoes you've been looking for. These are the shoes you'll wear every day, whether they're appropriate for your outfit or not. The shoes that will comfort you, the shoes that will make you happy. The shoes that will hold up during the winter rains. The shoes other blossom before giving him the boot. It takes that long for some guys to stop stuttering.

✦ If he's an American guy, do not sleep with him on the first date no matter how much you want to. Even American guys who sport goatees and liberal arts degrees from Bard College have a little Puritan man stiffly standing on their shoulder, whispering that it's fine to sow those wild oats now, but would you take this slut home to Mother? On the other hand, if he's European or Latin American, and you so desire, go for it. Bring condoms.

✦ The thing about watching how he treats his mother to see how he treats women in general? It's true. So observe carefully.

✦ Never date married men. No matter how good looking or charming or how incredibly they bonk. You can find someone single to have medicinal sex with and avoid the bad karma. Otherwise, what's the point? You want a relationship with a man who cheats on his wife?

✦ Avoid handsome Arab millionaires with fast-driving, wine-drinking, Prozac-taking chauffeurs.

chicks will comment on approvingly as you stand in line for your morning muffin.

Sadly, men sometimes are a bit more trying on your nerves than shoes. But there is nothing wrong with going barefoot while shopping.

Heartbreak

Sigh. You've been down this road before. And unlike most things in life, heartbreak doesn't get any easier with experience. You do, however, probably understand the heartbreak process much better than you did back at 16, when the pain of that first dumping was so great no one could convince you it wasn't terminal. You now know, for example, that for the first couple of days, it's simply a chemical imbalance that you're powerless against, so you must let yourself scream, cry, throw things at your walls, and burn the bastard in effigy. But after the first week, the healing process can start. And you know what to do to help that along.

- **Music management.** Avoid these songs at all costs:
  Sinead O'Connor's "Nothing Compares 2 U"
  Chris Isaak's "Wicked Game"
  Seal by Seal; the album
  "Your Song," by whoever
  Anything by Tori Amos

- **Shopping.** Go to the Goodwill. Buy $50 worth of retro clothes and other funky stuff. Even if you never wear most of it, you will feel better. If you're not the thrift-store type, and you have the cash, go to Nordstrom and buy the most expensive pair of shoes you like and refuse to feel guilty. Some chicks prefer expensive makeup. Some prefer books. Buy whatever makes you oddly content and at peace with the world, but buy something. And feel no guilt.

- **Smoking.** You really should stop. But you know that already. And all breakups immediately void your resolve to quit.

You're allowed a pack or two until you get him out of your mind.

- **Fantasy.** Go ahead and put your plans of revenge into your head. Hell, put them on paper. The truly vengeful can create a website dedicated to the humiliation and torment of your ex-lover, including a post that will take continuous suggestions on further degradations.

- **Support.** Your girlfriends should be equally versed in how to nurse you back to health by this time. When I found out my first love in high school had been doing me dirty, two of my best girlfriends immediately drove over, plied me with chocolate, and forced me to accompany them to a screening of *Porky's*. It worked, in its own crude way. But these days a sushi dinner, four rounds of drinks, and multiple viewings of *Thelma and Louise* work better.

- **Refocus.** Rechannel your bitterness into something more constructive. Learn origami. Take up rowing. Or do what Andrea McGinty did and start your own damn dating service.

Lunch Date

Andrea McGinty's fiancé walked out on her five weeks before the wedding. He called her up, told her he just couldn't go through with it, and that he was quitting his job as a real estate contractor to move to Los Angeles and become an actor. "He never even liked going to the movies," she says.

Not a very auspicious beginning to one's 30s, and not highly promising for the future of her love life. But McGinty, who at the time was a 29-year-old marketer for a large costume jewelry company, decided that the best way to get over the trauma of being dumped at the altar was to get back out into the dating pool as soon as she could pull herself off the floor and out of the fetal position.

But it was pretty ugly out there. As with a lot of busy career chicks, McGinty just wasn't meeting interesting men in her day-to-day grind, which called for spending most of her time on the road. Nor did she have much time to look farther afield. So she tried the next logical steps—personal ads and dating services. These proved less than romantic as well. One date she met through a personal ad was so bad she got up to leave before the date was over only to have the guy hurl their pizza at the wall behind them. A video dating service worker told her, "You're getting old, but you're still semiattractive."

"All of a sudden being single, and almost 30, was tough," she says. "What's out there compared to when you're 24 or 25 is a real shock. I was down to my friends, and they're like, 'I like Andrea. I like Bob. They both don't smoke. They're perfect for each other.' That's where I was at."

Her dates were so bad, in fact, that she started meeting them for lunch only, mostly so she'd have a polite out after only one hour, instead of having to endure a hell date into the wee hours when she'd rather be home in her socks and bathrobe.

Other dating services weren't much better. Nobody seemed to take any time to get to know their clients personally, relying instead on form questionnaires and photos. McGinty started daydreaming about her perfect dating situation—where two well-matched, civilized people could meet in a safe, professional, yet comfortable venue. Over lunch, for example. Then she got to thinking.

"It just hit me out of the blue," she says. "Why didn't I start that kind of dating service?" Wouldn't people pay, and pay well, to meet eligible, professional others this way? As proof of her hunch, she dragged a friend into a popular singles bar one night and regarded the lonely, beer-besotted masses. "See?" she said. "Look at how many people are here, and they don't want to be! Look at their eyes!" Her friend had to agree.

Oooh. She just knew it would work. McGinty had worked long enough as a marketer for a jewelry business to know the value of niche marketing. She paid for a list of names and addresses of the demographic she was after—single, professional types making 50K a year or more—the sort of folks who generally don't throw pizzas against the wall—and found that there were 150,000 of them living within the space of a half-hour walk from her. The market was there.

Then she took the next step: she quit her job and maxed out her credit card for $6,000 in cash advances. She rented a tiny office in downtown Chicago and made 20,000 brochures that she and girlfriends stuffed under these same genteel doors early one Sunday morning. It's Just Lunch was born.

As with all the best business ideas, this one was so simple it was scandalous to think nobody had done it before. McGinty would personally get to know each and every client before making a match. Once a good match was set on paper, she'd make reservations at an upscale restaurant near where both parties worked for a lunch date. If things worked out, the couple was free to make the second date and beyond. But if not, then it was just lunch, and one or the other was free to beg off to that all-important 2 P.M. meeting. Clients would then call her with feedback as to why it wasn't a love match, and next time she could set them up with someone more appropriate. Smaller nose, less perfume. Whatever.

To get started, McGinty gave several dozen of her single friends free memberships (to pay them back for some of the dates they set her up on?) and waited for that first call.

It was touch and go at first, she says. The very first person who called, a man, asked how many members she'd signed up. "You're the first," she admitted. He declined to sign on until she got a bit more established. The second person who called was a public relations consultant who offered to swap free PR for dates. "I didn't hesitate on that one," she laughs. She agreed, and in a few months, news about It's Just Lunch began appearing in local business magazines and newspapers. Her phone began to ring. Three months after she hung out her shingle, McGinty had more than 400 members, each of whom was paying $400 for a total of six dates.

Business was going great. But what of her personal life? "It mostly wasn't there," she says. "I was too busy growing my business." Well that's all fine and nice, but a gal needs a little romantic distraction now and then for health reasons. Friends tried to set her up, but McGinty didn't have the time. No, not even for lunch.

Then one day a young lawyer walked in wanting to sign up for her service. McGinty brought him in to the next room to fill out the questionnaire and be interviewed, trying to keep professional even though she herself thought he was a babe. After he'd gone out on two lunches he called her up to cancel his membership. "Why?" she wanted to know. "Did we do something wrong?" It wasn't that, he said. It was just that he'd met the perfect woman and he wouldn't need to use her services anymore. "That's great," said McGinty. "Who is she?"

"You," the lawyer said.

Well. That was flattering, sure. But McGinty knew a lot more about this guy, having interviewed him, than he knew about her. She told him as much.

That may be true, said the lawyer, but would she go out with him anyway? McGinty said no, of course not. Not company policy to date clients.

So the lawyer kept his membership for a few more months, but only until he came up with another way to ask McGinty out. This time, he said he had some professional business advice for her about how to grow her business. McGinty couldn't say no to that, but when they met again early one morning after their workouts (same gym, conveniently), he asked her out again. No way, she said. Why not? he countered.

She listed the reasons. They had nothing in common, this much she knew, she reminded him, because she had interviewed him. More important, he'd made it very clear in that interview that he was "opposed to the institution of marriage." She did want to get married one day, she told him, and even though it probably wouldn't be to him, why waste her time at all? "I was being surly with him because I just didn't care," admits McGinty. Besides, she was already seeing another promising man.

But this lawyer, being a lawyer, wasn't daunted. "Go home and at least consider going out with me," he said.

"No," said McGinty, who was tired of all this. "You go home and consider whether you ever want to get married or not."

He called her the next day and conceded. One day he probably would get married. One day. She agreed to give him one date.

Then a second date. On the third date, the lawyer proposed to her.

McGinty's been married to this guy for three years now. And her business is doing better than ever, opening offices all over the known universe. True, it is well-known dating lore that if you stop caring you'll meet someone right away, but here's one bona fide example of when this attitude actually worked.

Your Sexual Peak

You've been waiting a long time for this one, girlie. Ever since painfully losing it in the garage of your boyfriend's parents' house, you've been building up to this. Your whole sexual life you've been hearing tales of what happens to a woman's sexual drive once she reaches her 30s, and I don't have to tell you, some of those tales push the boundaries on natural limits. For some of us, the promise of reaching this sexual nirvana is the only thing that's kept us going.

It is a well-documented fact that women begin to get wild in their 30s and cannot find enough time in any given day to have as much sex as they want. I chalk this up to nature. Back in the caveman days, you'd proven your worth to the tribe by bearing many children and now that you were past that you'd earned the right to consort with the young bucks. Rather, they earned the right to consort with you, you fertile thing you. Nature must have decided that lusty older women would continue to breed if it felt better while doing it, and so provided forthwith.

Thirtyish women start reporting double, even serial orgasms with much less effort on their part. They whisper about the X-rated daydreams that suddenly hit them on the train ride home. They begin to mentally undress busboys. They secretly worry about becoming like men, so doglike are these strange new lusts. "If you ever wanted to experiment with new techniques or equipment, now's a good time to start," says Isadora Altman, the syndicated sexologist.

Sound good to you? Well, hold on there, missy. You're not at the peak of your sexual peak yet. That comes (quite explosively, I'm told), in your mid- to late 30s. As a mere initiate into the wonders of sexual freedom, you as a 30-year-old should simply strive to work on a good base. Never have the instructions to "practice, practice, practice" been more lustily meant. After all, how can you be a master if you haven't mastered the basics?

That means you've got to start thinking like the grown woman you are. First, you'll need to know what your limits are. Then you'll need the right equipment. Don't waste your time checking out a sex shop if anything other than the missionary pose strikes you as daring. Your own room is important, as is what I quaintly term a "fuck bed." This is the kind of large (queen- or king-size), clean, comfortable bed (or futon) found in the bedrooms of most single chicks in their 30s. When I was deciding whether to buy a bed or another futon after a move, a friend of mine once counseled, "Don't skimp on bedding. Sometimes it will be all there is to comfort you." This was very good advice, and because of it, I spent a bit more and ended up

with one of the most comfortable futons in Manhattan. Everyone who ever visited it remarked on its comforts, and I got a
very good night's sleep as well. Eventually, I mean.

Other implements you'll need to prepare for your sexual
peak:

A working shower

A reliable vibrator

A jar of condoms, all colors and flavors

Very simple, high-quality lingerie (for you, sister, not for
him)

I also suggest you read everything by Anaïs Nin, as well as
the entire *Beauty* series by A. N. Roquelaire (really, Anne
Rice). These can add *frisson* when there is none otherwise, or
at least enable you to spend a hot night with yourself. And God
knows we've had to get good at that, haven't we, girls?

A lot of your new sexual drive comes from all your newfound confidence. When you can take your clothes off in front
of a guy, knowing you don't possess the body of Pamela Lee, but
fully aware that most guys are too thrilled to care, then you
know you're on the threshold. How can you have monster sex
if you're too embarrassed he'll see your butt? No. You must truly
be comfortable with the body you have. And for a lot of American chicks, this takes 30 years to accomplish by itself. But
sooner or later you start to be comfortable with the body you
have, and then men start falling over themselves to talk to you
when you walk into a room. To dally with the sex goddesses,
you must think of yourself as a sex goddess, flat chest or no.

With the right equipment and the right attitude, you're
ready to enjoy sex like you've never enjoyed it before. Of
course, making the most of your sexual peak depends a lot on
what kind of chick you were in your 20s. Did your sole sexual

experience come from weekly two-minute quickies with your college boyfriend (in which case you have a lot of catching up to do), or were you more the "let-no-man-go-untasted" variety? If you can cite more than 20 names on your lover list, then now is the time for you to focus on quality rather than quantity. I suggest you, ah, specialize in a few subgenres. Conversely, if you're a delicate untasted flower, I suggest you get in touch with your inner slut.

I have a very good friend, a friend who would hunt me down and kill me if I gave her name and connected her in any way to the following anecdote. This girlfriend and I have known each other since our early 20s, when we met at our first job out of college. We routinely took long walks to get coffee any chance we got, and kvetched about what concerns most 22-year-olds: our low rate of pay, the slave conditions at work, our crappy roommates, and, of course, our boyfriends. Whenever the talk turned to sex, I would note uncomfortably that, whereas our views converged in most areas, they most certainly did not in this one. It was obvious that she had had two partners in her life whereas I'd had, ah, many more, and that my take on sex as sport was one she didn't share.

Jump-start ten years later. We're still good friends. After moving cross-country and back again, we've found ourselves in the same town again. She is telling me about a guy she's known a long time, sort of a family friend. She tells me that she and he and a group of other friends went out last night, and that at the end of the evening, it was just he and she together, and somehow they just ended up, you know, together. "So you guys had a nice snuggle," I say, gathering, from conversations past, that she'd never go further than that with a guy she hadn't been dating for weeks. "Oh no," she said, matter-of-factly.

"I had to get laid. He spent the night." Well, didn't that just raise my eyebrows. Seems my friend had undergone her own sexual metamorphosis, caused by years of experience, increased confidence in herself, and, presumably, heightened insight into the ways of men.

Chances are, if you're even approaching 30 you've noticed a change in the temperature when it comes to what you want out of sex. Everyone grows bolder with experience, but it's a hormonal thing too. What once might have left you squeamish now prompts you to fall off your chair with lust. It's nature just reinforcing the larger picture—that everything in your life, from the orgasms to your orzo mystery dish, is only going to get better from here. And Mother Nature would know, wouldn't she?

So go to it, girlfriend. Go to town. Leave no rock unturned. Think of dating in your 30s as one big dangerous liaison (without the wigs—unless you're into that). You're old enough and wise enough to introduce as much intrigue as possible into your affairs of the heart, and you're old enough to cop the responsibility for your actions. Just don't be stupid about any of this. If you've come this far disease-free, now is no time to learn about new and incurable diseases. You *are* old enough to know better about some things.

FAMOUS LAST WORDS

The answering machine turned 30 in 1997. Instant coffee turned 30 in 1998. No doubt a lot of you are about to turn 30 yourselves, if you haven't already. I don't have to tell you that the answering machine has become a device no girl could live without, just as everyone has a jar of Folgers mountain-grown in the cupboard in case there should ever be a Starbucks boycott. My point? You're still relevant, baby. But you tell me—what's your prognosis right about now?

I hope it involves none of the hand-wringing of your late 20s. Yeah, it made for good drama and, yes, perhaps it was appropriate at the time, but where did all that worrying get you? It got you to 30. And now everything's much better, right? Of course right. The truth is, there just isn't a downside to this turning-30 business.

I hope you can see all of this clearly now. I hope you're finding out for yourself that being a chick in your early 30s is like your best summer ever: lots of neato projects, good food, challenging hikes. Maybe even a Ken doll.

When all those women cornered me in my office the week before my 30th birthday and told me life would be picking up soon, I didn't believe them. When they insisted that great things would happen between 30 and 33, I shook my head and stomped my feet. No! Not for me it wouldn't. I was too far gone. Too wretched. Too unhappy too much of the time.

But they were right. Life picked up. It simply started when I stopped trying to be who I thought I should be and gave in to my proclivity toward mismatched clothing and Birkenstocks, toward just being befuddled, bookish J. T., and not some faux Manhattan power chick who scared her parents. After cracking that nut I started liking myself again after years of not liking myself very much. Funny, but everything else seems to have hinged on that one point.

Here's another funny thing: it keeps getting better.

No, not better in that glassy-eyed, New Age way. This is still life we're talking about here. Your rent checks may still bounce. Your career plans may yet go up in smoke. Your car may still be stolen even though you spent all that money on the Lo-Jack. It gets better because every year you live life after 30 fills up your glass a little more, and you're the richer for it. You can finally see that at 20 you didn't even know where your glass was. Every chick I talked to about turning 30 agreed on one point: no way in hell would they ever want to be 22 again. No matter what. That alone should make you feel righteous.

I dig being 33. It really is an almost perfect age. I'm not too young and I'm not too old. It's as if I'm straddling the parallel universes of foolish youth and rational adulthood, but I can step over into either whenever I feel like it, without feeling like too much of a fraud. Staying out all night is no longer my idea of a fun evening, but once you got me out there I'd probably be the one still dancing on the bar at dawn.

You're going to like being 30 yourself. Trust me on this one, OK? Everything starts the morning of your 30th birthday, when you wake up and wonder what all the fuss was about. Then you simply roll up your sleeves (or shake out your futon, depending on what you were up to that night), and resolve to get a fresh start.

I hope I was able to calm down a few souls with some of this. I've always found that nothing helps better than empathy. And as you've probably guessed by now, I'll empathize with almost anyone who will have me.

OK. Time to put this bitch session to bed. I can't possibly have another coffee. I've already had to get up 15 times to pee and people are staring. I had a great time, and I hope you did too.

Let's do it again when we're all 39 and counting.

READING FOR CHICKS

Don't find yourself without these books on your bookshelf, lady. These are just a meager start, of course, on your way to chick literacy. But feel free to explore and expand as time and money allow.

Divided Lives, Elsa Walsh (Anchor, 1995). Proof you can't have it all. Not all at once.

Fear of Flying, Erica Jong (Signet, 1974). Adventures of an almost-30 chick 20 years ago.

The Feminine Mystique, Betty Friedan (Dell, 1963). You can't know where you're going if you don't know where you've been.

The Fountain of Age, Betty Friedan (Simon & Schuster, 1993). Everything you ever wanted to know about aging, but didn't know where to start.

Get a Financial Life: Personal Finance in Your Twenties and Thirties, Beth Kobliner (Fireside, 1996). A good primer for when you're ready to finally learn what a no-load mutual fund is.

The Good Vibrations Book of Good Sex, Cathy Winks and Anne Semans (Cleis Press, 1994). Read it, learn it, live it. Then get on the mailing list.

Just who the Hell is SHE, Anyway?, Marisa Acocella (Harmony, 1994). The chick who drew the wicked "SHE" cartoon in *Mirabella* does a book. And it's all about *us*!

Marriage Shock, Dalma Heyn (Villard, 1997). Yikes! And you wanted to get married? Read this first.

Red Hot Mamas: Coming into Our Own at Fifty, Colette Dowling (Bantam, 1996). May bring insights into your mother and her generation.

A Room of One's Own, Virginia Woolf (Harcourt Brace Jovanovich, 1929). Good advice for creative women that still holds true nearly 70 years later.

The Seasons of a Woman's Life, Daniel J. Levinson (Knopf, 1996). Real insights from a guy who'd know.

The Second Sex, Simone de Beauvoir (Vintage, 1952). You can't really call yourself a chick until you've dug on Simone. Required reading.

Sex Tips for Girls, Cynthia Heimel (Fireside, 1983). The book all other chick books are based on. And probably the funniest book you'll ever read.

A Woman's Book of Life, Joan Borysenko, Ph.D. (Riverhead, 1996). A pleasing read that makes you feel like part of the circle. For once.

ABOUT THE AUTHOR

J ulie Tilsner is in her mid-30s and is handling it fine so far. She's still paying off the student loans for her year at Columbia University's Graduate School of Journalism but hopes to be debt-free by her mid-40s. She's a former assistant editor at *Business Week Magazine* and has written for a number of other publications as well, including the *New York Times*, the *Los Angeles Times*, *Lingua Franca*, *P.O.V.*, *Working Woman*, and *Women's Wire*, an on-line magazine. She lives in San Francisco with her husband and baby daughter and entertains dreams of fitting once again into the diet skirt.